ROCK**RHYTHM**
GUITAR**PLAYING**

The Complete Rock Guitar Rhythm Method

JOSEPH**ALEXANDER**

FUNDAMENTAL**CHANGES**

Rock Rhythm Guitar Playing

Published by **www.fundamental-changes.com**

ISBN: 978-1-78933-063-2

Published by **www.fundamental-changes.com**

www.fundamental-changes.com

Twitter: @guitar_joseph

Over 10,000 fans on Facebook: **FundamentalChangesInGuitar**

Instagram: **FundamentalChanges**

For over 350 Free Guitar Lessons with Videos Check Out

www.fundamental-changes.com

Cover Image Copyright: ShutterStock / mrkornflakes

Other Books from Fundamental Changes

100 Classic Rock Licks for Guitar

Beyond Rhythm Guitar

Complete Technique for Modern Guitar

Exotic Pentatonic Soloing for Guitar

First Chord Progressions for Guitar

Funk Guitar Mastery

Guitar Chords in Context

Guitar Fretboard Fluency

Guitar Scales in Context

Heavy Metal Guitar Bible

Heavy Metal Lead Guitar

Heavy Metal Rhythm Guitar

Progressive Metal Guitar

Rock Guitar Un-CAGED

Rock Rhythm Guitar Playing

The Circle of Fifths for Guitarists

The Complete DADGAD Guitar Method

The Complete Guide to Playing Blues Guitar Book One: Rhythm Guitar

The Complete Guide to Playing Blues Guitar Book Three: Beyond Pentatonics

The Complete Guide to Playing Blues Guitar Book Two: Melodic Phrasing

The Complete Guide to Playing Blues Guitar Compilation

The Complete Technique, Theory & Scales Compilation for Guitar

The First 100 Chords for Guitar

The Practical Guide to Modern Music Theory for Guitarists

Rock Guitar Mode Mastery

NeoClassical Speed Strategies for Guitar with Chris Brooks

Sweep Picking Speed Strategies for Guitar with Chris Brooks

Advanced Arpeggio Soloing for Guitar

Contents

Introduction 5

Get the Audio 7

Part One: The Building Blocks of Rock Rhythm Guitar 8

Chapter One: Understanding Rhythm 9

Chapter Two: Rests, Ties and Combinations 16

Chapter Three: 1/16th Note Rhythm Combinations 22

Chapter Four: 1/16th Note Rests 28

Chapter Five: Single Note Groupings 36

Part Two: Chords, Riffs and Music 40

Chapter Six: Rock Guitar Chords 41

Chapter Seven: Embellishments 53

Chapter Eight: Barre Chords and Single Lines 63

Classic Rock Style File 75

Chapter Nine: Rock Rhythm Guitar through the Decades 76

    The 1950s 76

    The 1960s 78

    The 1970s 80

    The 1980s 83

    The 1990s 85

    The 2000s 88

    The 2010s 91

Conclusions and Practice Advice 103

Conclusions and Practice Advice 93

Appendix: Advanced Rhythm Exercises 95

Other Books from Fundamental Changes 99

Introduction

Rock music encompasses a huge range of genres, sounds and styles. From the beginnings of rock n' roll in the late 50s to the heavy metal of the 80s, through to modern day Indie and Alternative rock, the guitar is always at the forefront and cutting edge of the style.

Mastering the rhythmic skills and techniques required to play rock guitar will also answer questions about how to play solid rhythm guitar parts in any other style of music.

This book is split into two parts and you should work through both parts at the same time. Part One covers everything you need to know about understanding rhythm and building tight, solid rock grooves from first principles. In this section you will learn how rhythm functions in music, and from these basic building blocks you will quickly learn to put together exciting and detailed rhythm guitar parts. In Part One, you will build your guitar technique and theoretical understanding of how rhythm functions on the guitar while also mastering its performance.

By building from first principles you will never be confused about how a rhythm should be executed on the guitar. By developing confidence and consistency at this stage you'll find it simple to speed up any riff you're playing to the standards required by fast, modern rock music.

The aim of Part One is to solidify a consistent and accurate approach to playing rock rhythm guitar. This will be extremely beneficial to you, whatever style of music you play.

In Part One, we will also look at building a repertoire of important chord types and variations that are commonly used to build riffs and musical ideas in rock guitar. We will study how to use open chords, power chords, and full and partial barre chords. We will then look at how to combine these chord ideas with single note riffs to construct interesting and intricate rock guitar parts.

Part Two takes a detailed look at how rock guitar has developed over the past fifty years. It contains many actual riffs inspired by the greatest bands of each decade. This is where the theory and technique are put into practice to create musical examples that consolidate the skills developed in Part One.

'In the style of' riffs are given for every important rock guitar movement, from rockabilly to '80s shred. Modern 'Indie' examples are included as well as the defining rock classics of the '60s and '70s.

Rock guitar can be a technically demanding genre, so to help you develop your skills more quickly, I recommend that this book is used in conjunction with my other bestselling guitar guide **Complete Technique for Modern Guitar**. I highly recommend that you work through the sections in Complete Technique alongside this book to build your technique and get the most out of the rock riffs and concepts taught here.

The idea behind **Rock Rhythm Guitar** is simple: to combine rhythmic technique and understanding with chord knowledge in Part One, before turning these skills into practical music in Part Two. There is no need to work through this book in order and I highly encourage you work through Part One and Part Two at the same time.

Each exercise in this book is accompanied by an audio example that can be downloaded for free from **www.fundamental-changes.com**. I recommend that you go there now to get the audio as it will help you learn and understand each example much more quickly. Simply click on the 'Download Audio' tab and select this book from the dropdown menu.

Download the audio to your PC (not directly to your iPad, Kindle or phone). Extract the audio from the .zip file and then import it to your media library. It's really simple and there's a help guide on the download page if you get stuck.

Learning music is all about *hearing* how the music should sound. Sometimes it is impossible to show the nuance and feel of the music when it is written down in tablature and notation, so I highly recommend listening to the audio to get the most out of the 152 examples in this book.

The audio download also contains essential backing tracks that allow you to play along with the examples while helping you develop a great rock guitar feel.

The concept behind this book is to help you master and internalise the essential skills in rock guitar, and learn to see how these fundamental building blocks have been used to form some of the most important riffs and songs of the last hundred years. Once mastered, these building blocks will allow you to quickly learn, assimilate or *create* any rock guitar music that you hear in your head.

Have fun!

Joseph

Get the Audio

The audio files for this book are available to download for free from www.fundamental-changes.com. The link is in the top right-hand corner. Simply select this book title from the drop-down menu and follow the instructions to get the audio.

We recommend that you download the files directly to your computer, not to your tablet, and extract them there before adding them to your media library. You can then put them on your tablet, iPod or burn them to CD. On the download page there is a help PDF and we also provide technical support via the contact form.

For over 350 Free Lessons with Videos Check out:

www.fundamental-changes.com

Over 10,000 fans on Facebook: **FundamentalChangesInGuitar**

Instagram: **FundamentalChanges**

Part One: The Building Blocks of Rock Rhythm Guitar

Chapter One: Understanding Rhythm

The majority of rock rhythm guitar parts are formed from 1/4 note, 1/8th note and 1/16th note (crotchet, quaver and semiquaver) rhythmic divisions. It is essential to develop understanding and control of how these patterns function and feel in order to produce authentic and accurate guitar parts.

The exercises in this chapter begin in a straightforward manner, although you will quickly learn how they can become intricate, powerful and musical.

We begin by examining how to build rhythm guitar parts from the ground up, and work towards playing accurate and musical combinations of any rhythm on the guitar. As we start to add chords to these rhythmic ideas the music suddenly becomes alive with possibilities.

1/16th notes, as the name suggests, divide one bar (or 'measure') of music into sixteen equal parts. There are four equal divisions of a beat in a bar containing four beats. 1/16th notes are the smallest common division of the beat in rock rhythm guitar and our eventual rhythmic goal. When we can understand, feel and *play* any 1/16th note rhythm, we know that we have formed a solid rhythmic foundation for anything that follows.

Before playing 1/16th notes, we will develop accuracy with smaller subdivisions of the beat (1/4 and 1/8th notes) so that we can master the placement of each rhythmic level.

In rock music, the majority of the rhythms you will play will be based on 1/4 note and 1/8th note combinations. 1/16th note rhythms appear more in *heavier* rock rhythms (think Van Halen through to Metallica), so in terms of your development as a guitarist, view working towards accurate 1/16th note rhythms as an extra layer of technical proficiency you should attain.

You will tend to play more 1/16th note if you're into the heavier side of rock, but even if you're not, 1/16th notes are still an essential component of any great rock guitar player's arsenal.

We will begin by dividing a single bar (or 'measure') of music into four even beats (1/4 notes). The accurate execution of this rhythm may seem simple, but it is fundamental to everything you will ever play on the guitar.

In the following example, pay attention to the strumming directions written under each note. Building consistency in the strumming hand is extremely important because it allows us to accurately keep time and feel exactly where we are in the bar.

It is worth pointing out that any rhythmic chord idea can also be used as a rhythm in a guitar solo.

Listen to Example 1a before playing along with the recording.

Example 1a:

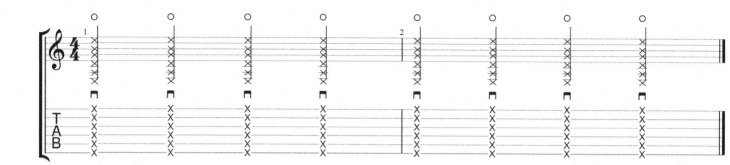

Mute the strings of the guitar with your fretting hand in order to create a scratch or 'thwack' sound. This can be achieved by lightly resting the fingers of the fretting hand across all six strings to kill the sound.

Avoid pressing too heavily on the strings otherwise you will create undesired ringing notes. Also, be careful to avoid creating *harmonics* by accidentally pressing lightly over the 5th or 7th fret. Aim to create a dead, muted sound so that you can accurately hear where each strum is falling.

Play Example 1a with a metronome set to 60bpm. The small circles above each strum represent the metronome click. Make sure that every down-strum is perfectly in time with the click. This can be deceptively tricky at first. Focusing your ears on the click rather than your strum can help a great deal.

Now, divide each down-strum (1/4 note) into two, thereby creating 1/8th notes. To do this, add an even up-strum in between each down-strum. Again, the small circle represents the metronome click and every down-strum should sync perfectly with the click. The up-strum should be placed exactly halfway between each down-strum.

Example 1b:

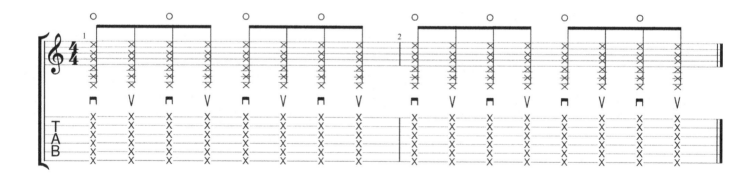

Try Exercise 1b at different speeds. Begin at 60bpm and gradually work your way up to 120bpm, gradually increasing the metronome speed by about 8bpm whenever you start to feel comfortable. The key is to *listen* to the placement of your down-strum. It should always sync perfectly with the metronome click.

Next, try reducing the metronome speed to 40bpm or below. Playing accurately at a slow tempo is more challenging than at faster tempos because we have to mentally divide a greater stretch of time.

Finally, move on to playing 1/16th note divisions of the bar by 'doubling up' the strums in the previous example. You are now playing *four strums per metronome click.*

Begin with the metronome set at 60bpm and concentrate on placing the *first* of each group of four strums directly on the click. You play one sequence of *downupdownup* for each metronome click.

Try to accent the first of each four strums by hitting it slightly harder. This will help you to stay in time.

Listen carefully to the audio example to get a feel for this and to check your accuracy.

Example 1c:

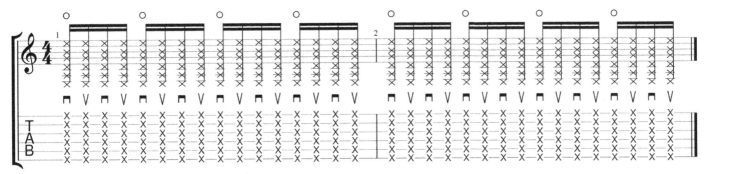

As your accuracy begins to improve, increase the metronome speed in increments of 8bpm and gradually work your way up to 120bpm, although you should never sacrifice accuracy for speed. If the tempo is too challenging, slow down a little bit and work in short bursts to develop your endurance.

Also build your accuracy by reducing the metronome speed back down to 50 or even 40bpm. Playing more slowly requires more control and focus, so it is a great way to build proficiency.

Next, repeat the previous three exercises but this time, instead of strumming a single muted string, play each rhythm with a single 'power chord'. (See Chapter Six for much more information about power chords).

Power chords will be discussed in detail later, but for now make sure that you only hit the strings indicated on the chord grid and notation. If you like, you can mute the guitar strings slightly by allowing the 'heel' (skin) of your picking hand to slightly touch the strings next to the bridge of the guitar.

Notice that playing fretted notes feels slightly different to playing muted strings so it needs to be practiced separately. You also can experiment by varying the pressure of your fretting hand to create more or less muted notes.

When playing the following few examples, dial in a little bit of gain (crunch) to your amp to help you learn to deal with an amp that is slightly distorting. Keep the distortion subtle, and experiment with your picking hand muting position to keep the sound articulate and defined.

Example 1d:

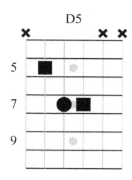

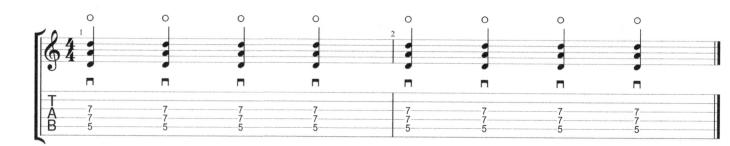

When playing rock guitar rhythms, there are two ways to approach playing consistent 1/8th notes. The first, as you might expect, is to use the most technically 'obvious' approach and play the 1/8th notes with alternating down- and up-strums as we did in Example 1b. This is shown below:

Example 1e:

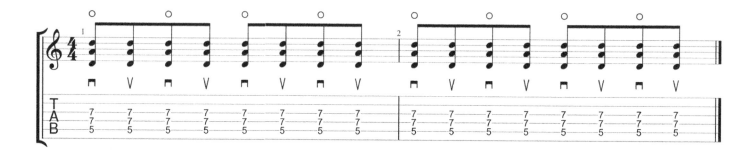

However… an extremely important concept to understand is that rhythm guitarists tend to feel 1/8th note divisions as the strongest rhythms in a song.

The drums and other instruments will accent the main 1/4 note pulse of 1, 2, 3, 4, but rock guitarists tend to 'lock in' to the 1/8th note pulse of the song and use it as their basic division. Listen to early Black Sabbath to get a feel for this. The main verse riff in *Paranoid* is a great example.

For this reason, guitarists often play every 1/8th note as a down-strum and this contributes a great deal to the driving 1/8th note rhythms of rock.

Example 1f:

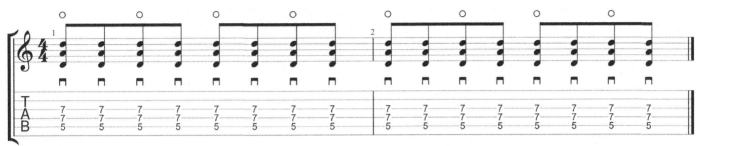

Compare how it feels to play the previous two examples by playing along with backing track one and notice the different feel that is created in each example.

The way you strum a rhythm pattern will often depend on the tempo and style of the song, but most rock guitarists play continuous 1/8th note rhythms with all down-strums just like in Example 1f.

When we move to 1/16th note divisions, most players will play them as alternating down- and up-strums (although many modern 'Thrash' and 'Death' Metal players will play 1/16ths with exclusively down-strums). For now I suggest that you stick to alternate strumming with 1/16th note rhythms.

When playing 1/16th note rhythms, it is easy for the notes to blend into an undefined mess (especially when playing with distortion). Be sure to use some light palm muting to help articulate each strum.

Practice the example below to develop tight, 1/16th note rhythm playing.

Example 1g:

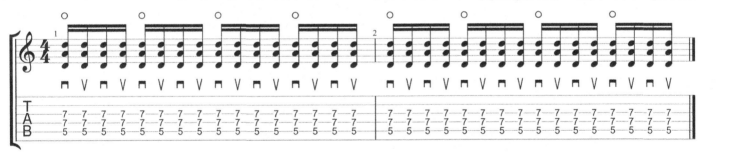

To continue building accuracy, and to practice moving between different rhythmic levels, try the following exercise that shifts between 1/4, 1/8 and 1/16th notes.

Example 1h:

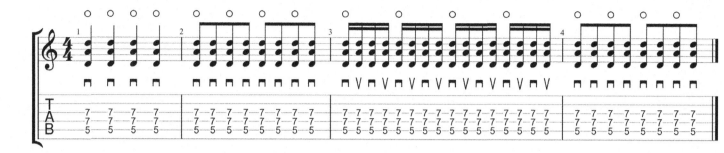

To help control your pick and improve your accuracy, try resting the heel of your picking hand on the lower (unused) strings of the guitar. Keep the tension in your picking hand as light and relaxed as possible, but be aware of the skin of the heel of the hand continually brushing the sixth and fifth strings to dampen them.

The secret to building accuracy in this kind of exercise is to focus more on the metronome click than the sound of the guitar. If you shift your attention to the metronome, you will find yourself playing more in time. This is also true when playing with a band: by focusing on the rhythm and music of others, we can often find ourselves playing much more in the pocket of the groove.

Also, it may not look cool, but tapping your foot on the beat will quickly help you internalise the rhythmic divisions and build your sense of time.

Next, increase the frequency at which you change rhythmic divisions.

Example 1i:

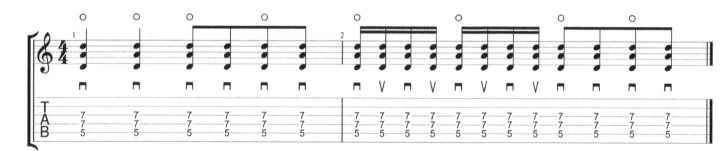

Try combining different rhythmic subdivisions and adding power chords to make the line musical.

Example 1j:

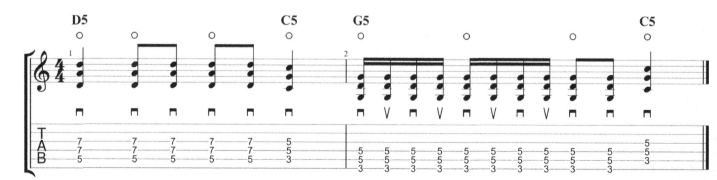

Example 1k:

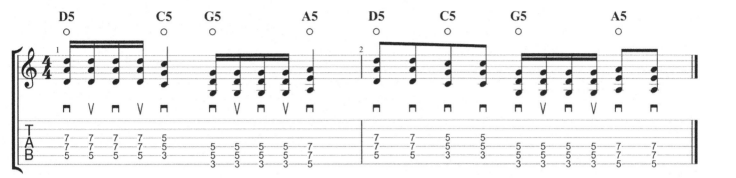

Practice the two previous exercises at 60bpm and gradually increase the metronome speed up to 120bpm.

The best piece of advice I can give you for learning these kinds of rhythms is to make sure that your foot is tapping on the beat. Tapping your foot helps you feel the beat physically, rather than just mentally responding to sound waves travelling through the air.

By internalising the beat physically you can *think* less about rhythm and *feel* whether you're in time.

If it's too much mental work to play these rhythms while tapping your foot while staying in time with the metronome, turn the metronome off for a while. Without the metronome, make sure that the strums on the guitar are falling in time with your foot. When you're confident, reintroduce the metronome at about 40bpm and sync your foot and strumming up with the click.

When I was first learning, it took me a long time to realise that my foot was out of time with the click, and this negatively affected *everything* I played on the guitar. When I put some serious concentration into my foot, my sense of rhythm improved dramatically. It's a very worthwhile use of your practice time and has far-reaching benefits to everything you play.

In order to practice these fundamental rock rhythms, write some of your own using the subdivisions that you have learned in this chapter. Try adding different power chords to create your own unique riffs.

By combining these rhythms, you will start to hear how a rock guitar part is built, although there is much more to developing your rhythmic feel than just these basic rhythms.

Chapter Two: Rests, Ties and Combinations

Often rock rhythm guitar involves playing *syncopated* rhythms. A syncopated rhythm is one where the stresses fall *between* the main pulses of the bar.

In Chapter One, you developed a consistent approach to strumming and I stressed that building consistency of the *downupdownup* 1/16th note strum pattern allows you to feel and place rhythms in the bar.

This consistency becomes very important now as we look at playing more intricate rhythms. Without a regular *downupdownup* in the picking hand it is easy to lose the rhythm and fall out of time with the band. Think of the strumming hand as your own personal conductor.

Rests

By using rests (beats of silence) and ties (combining the values of two notes), we can create complex rock guitar parts quite easily.

The first type of rest to introduce is the 1/8th note rest. It is written like this:

7

By placing this rest on a down beat, we can leave a rhythmic 'hole' in the guitar part. These holes help to create interesting syncopations and musical variation.

From the previous chapter, you know that a note falling on the beat is always played with a down-strum and that the secret to playing accurate rock rhythm guitar is always to keep your strumming hand moving up and down in time with the music. Even if you're not making contact with the strings, 'ghosting' with your strumming hand is essential for keeping good time.

Study the strumming directions in the following example to see how a syncopated 1/8th note pattern is played.

Example 2a:

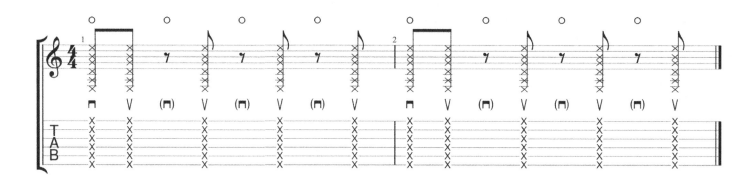

As you can see, there are 1/8th note rests on some of the down beats. The strumming direction underneath the example shows the down-strum written in brackets. If a strum is in brackets, do not make contact with the strings.

The idea is to keep the strumming hand moving up and down in time and simply to *miss* the strings whenever there is a rest. Listen carefully to the audio example to hear this in action.

Next, we will add power chords to the previous rhythm to show how an idea like this might be played in a musical rock context.

Begin with the metronome set to around 50bpm.

For this example I have reverted back to a 'down up' strum on the first two 1/8th note strums of the bar. Although this may seem to contradict the advice in the previous section about playing each 1/8th note as a down-strum, when the rhythm is syncopated like this a constant down up movement in the strumming hand really helps to keep time. Learn the rhythm with this strumming pattern for now, and decide how you want to strum it once you have mastered the feel of the exercise.

Example 2b:

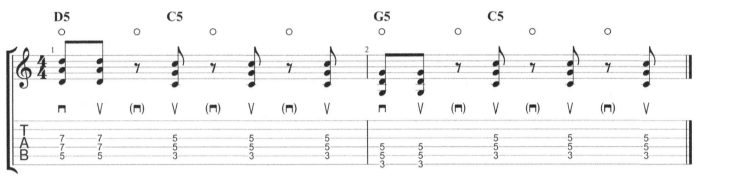

Here are some other riffs that combine 1/4 notes, 1/8th notes and 1/8th note rests.

Practice playing through each rhythm using muted 'scratched' strums before adding in the notated chords. Use palm, and fretting hand muting to help articulate the chords and rests.

These examples are similar to many '80s and '90s rock riffs. The simple introduction of 1/8th note rests into a power chord sequence really helps the riff to become alive.

Example 2c:

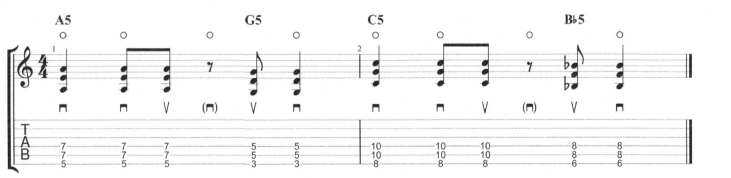

Example 2d:

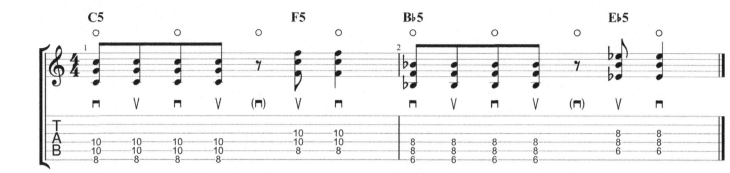

Example 2e:

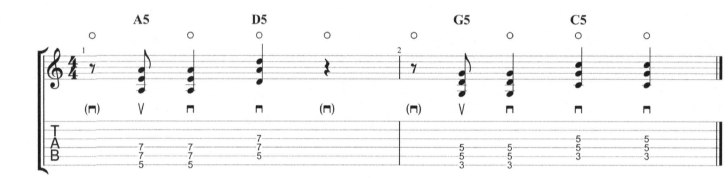

Practice speeding up and slowing down the previous examples. Use either a metronome or backing track one.

Ties

In music, a tie is a symbol that means 'play the first note and hold it for the value of the second note'.

It is written like this:

In the following example, play the first note of each tied pair but don't play the second one. Pay attention to the strumming pattern, and in particular the strums that are ghosted (shown in brackets).

Example 2f:

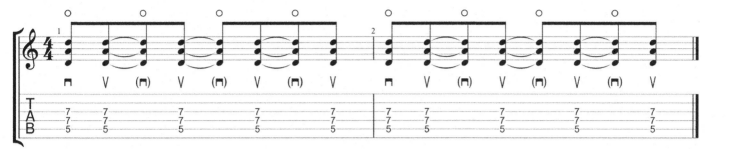

Listen to, and play along with the audio example to make sure that your playing is accurate.

There is a big difference between using ties and using rests depending on whether we are playing ringing chords or muted notes.

The following example shows the previous rhythm written with rests instead of ties.

Example 2g:

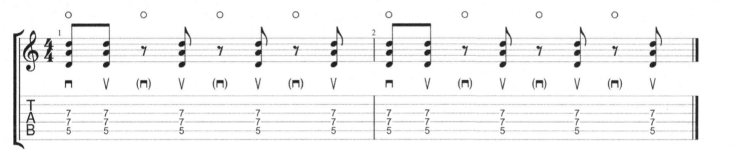

As you can hear in the audio example, these two rhythms have a very different feel even though the strums are in the same place.

The difference between playing a rest and a tie can have far-reaching effects on the groove of the music that we play.

Ties can allow us to move a chord *forward* in a riff. For example, they can be used to move a chord change *before* a bar line.

Examine the following two examples and listen carefully to the audio tracks.

Example 2h:

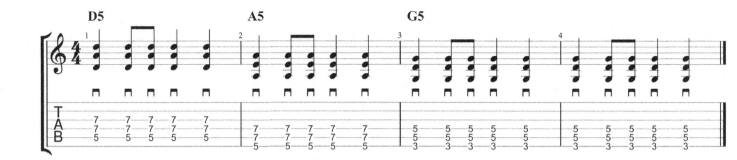

Example 2i:

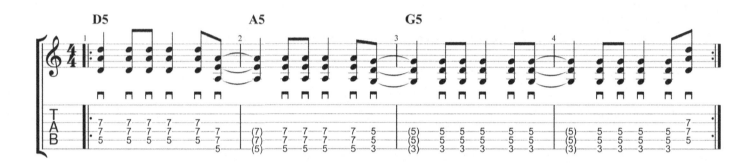

Both of these examples use the same chord progression and are played at the same tempo with very similar strumming patterns, but the second example has much more energy and forward momentum.

This extra energy has been created by playing each new chord an 1/8th note earlier. Each chord change is played on the final 1/8th note of the bar and is tied to beat one of the next bar. Not only does this add energy and forward movement, but it also creates an interesting rhythmic 'hole' on beat one of bars two, three and four where you would normally expect a chord to be placed.

Using ties in this way adds great interest and energy to rock riffs. Make sure that the bass player and drummer know that this is going to happen so that you can rhythmically lock in together.

Most rock musicians would describe this technique as *pushing* each chord, because each chord is 'pushed' an 1/8th note forward in the song. (Classical musicians call this technique 'anticipation'). Different bands push chords to a greater or lesser extent. For example, you hear a lot of pushed chords in AC/DC songs but less in the music of Black Sabbath.

The following three musical examples combine the techniques shown in this chapter.

Example 2j:

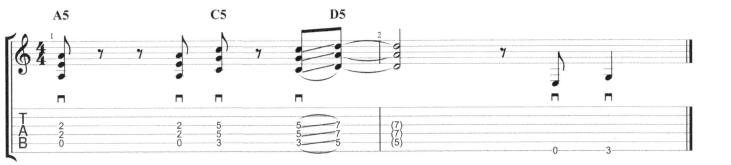

Notice the sliding chord in Example 2j leading to the D5 chord tied across the bar line.

Example 2k:

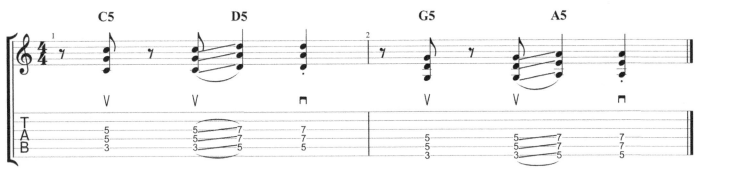

Example 2l:

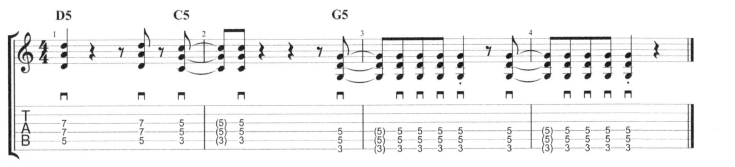

Don't forget, you can download all the audio examples for this book from:

www.fundamental-changes.com.

Chapter Three: 1/16th Note Rhythm Combinations

Now you have an understanding of how ties and rests work with 1/8th note rhythms, you can start to use them with the 1/16th note divisions that are common in modern rock guitar parts.

Let's explore what happens when you start using ties to join together 1/16th notes.

Remember; a tie indicates that you play the first note and continue to hold it for the value of the second, tied note.

In the following example, I play continuous 1/16th notes for one bar and then tie together the first two 1/16th notes in each beat. My right hand does not stop moving up and down during the tied rhythm.

The following examples are notated using a single note for clarity in the diagrams. However, you should begin with fully muted strums as using a large movement will help you to be more accurate.

Example 3a:

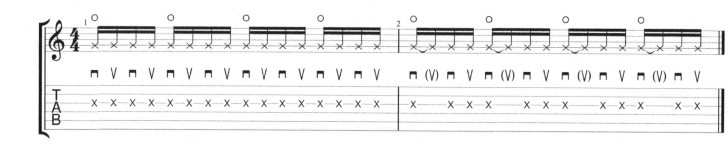

Listen to the audio and play through the exercise until you feel confident.

Tying together two 1/16th notes is mathematically the same as playing one 1/8th note (1/16 + 1/16 = 1/8).

This means that the previous example can be rewritten in the following way:

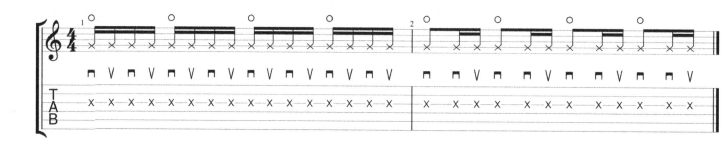

Although the previous two examples sound identical, you will probably find the second one easier to read.

Notice that the picking/strumming pattern is identical.

By tying together different 1/16th notes we can create some of the most commonly used rhythms in music.

In the next example, the *middle* two 1/16th notes are tied together in the second bar. Remember to play these examples with fully muted strums across all the strings. Don't just play the single strings that are notated.

Example 3b:

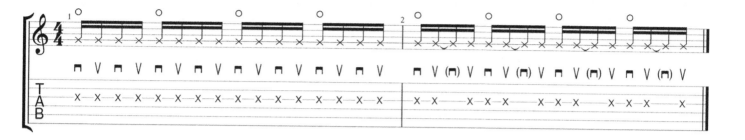

Again, the picking hand keeps moving *downupdownup*, but this time you miss out the second *down* of each group: *"Downup upDownup up"*.

Here is the same diagram without the bracketed picks. You may find it clearer to read:

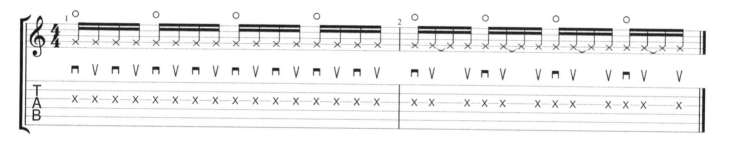

Applying the same logic as we did in Example 3a, this exercise can be rewritten as:

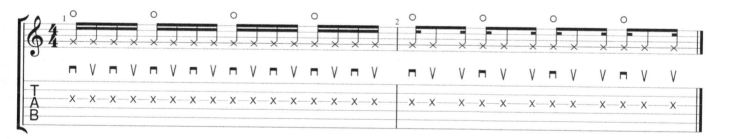

Play along with the audio track and make sure you tap your foot to the beat. It can be easy to get on the wrong side of these rhythms.

Finally (for now), tie together the final two 1/16th notes of each beat.

Example 3c:

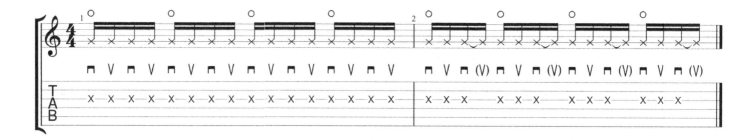

This can be written as:

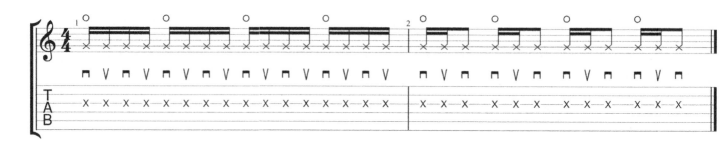

By tying together different pairs of 1/16th notes, we have created four different rhythmic groupings.

By combining these four 1/16th note rhythmic groupings, it is possible to create some extremely intricate rock guitar rhythms.

The combinations of these rhythms are virtually limitless, especially when you consider that we can also reintroduce rests to the phrases.

Before moving on, make sure you can play, recognise and read the four fundamental rhythmic building blocks of rock guitar shown in Example 3d:

Example 3d:

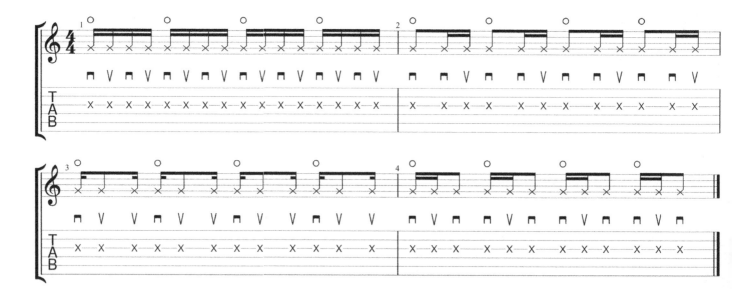

Play through Example 3d using fully muted strums before playing the exercise on a single muted string.

Now that you have mastered the four main 1/16th note patterns, combine them into one-bar phrases. The following examples reintroduce power chords to make the rhythms musical and more interesting, although you may once again find it easier to start with muted strums as you master the rhythmic combinations.

Use palm muting to help you hear the rhythms more clearly.

Example 3e combines just two of the previous rhythms.

Example 3e:

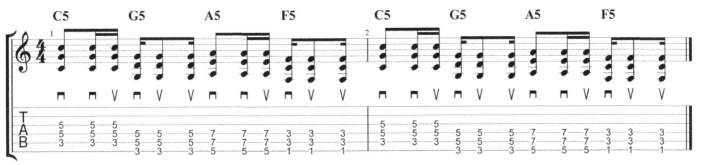

Example 3f combines three 1/16th note groupings.

Example 3f:

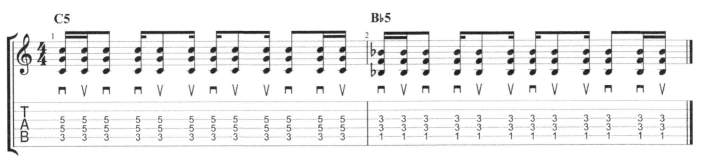

Example 3g uses the same three groupings in a different way.

Example 3g:

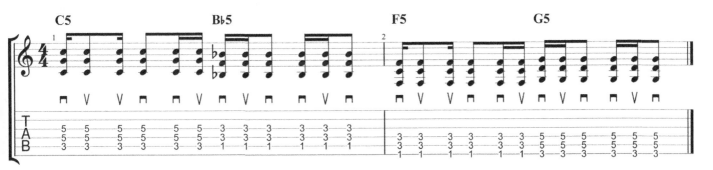

Example 3h uses all four 1/16th note groupings. Use heavy distortion and palm muting for a heavy metal vibe.

Example 3h:

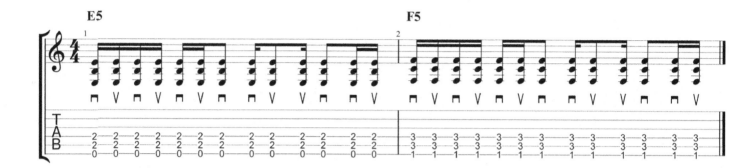

Example 3i shows another approach.

Example 3i:

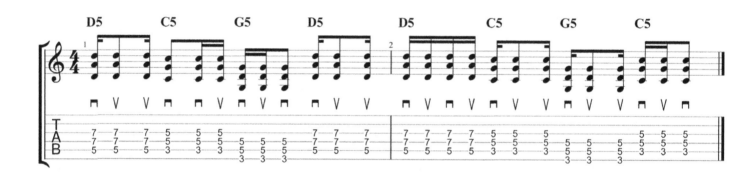

Finally, Example 3j reintroduces 1/8th note rests.

Example 3j:

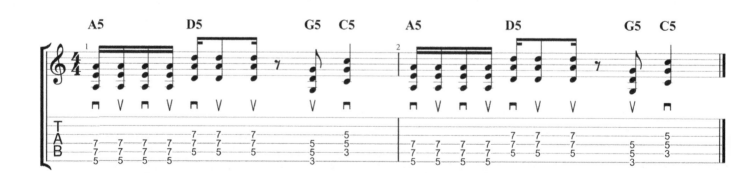

Important Note

In the previous example, you may find that the 1/8th note in beat three feels more natural as a down-strum. This is absolutely fine as long as you stay in time. The following might be more comfortable:

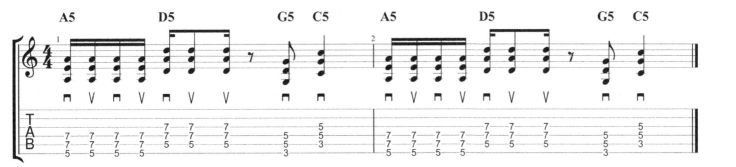

My advice is to go with whatever feels the most comfortable as long as you stick to it. Consistency in your strumming approach is incredibly important as you build up your rhythmic vocabulary.

With different strumming directions, you will find you end up with slightly different feels. Eventually you will be able to vary the attack at will, so don't worry too much about it for now.

Make sure you're tapping your foot in time and that you emphasise the difference between the chords and the rests. This can be achieved by careful control of the pressure in the fretting hand.

Chapter Four: 1/16th Note Rests

So far, we have studied four common 1/16th note groupings and how they can be combined to create interesting rock guitar riffs.

These four rhythms are:

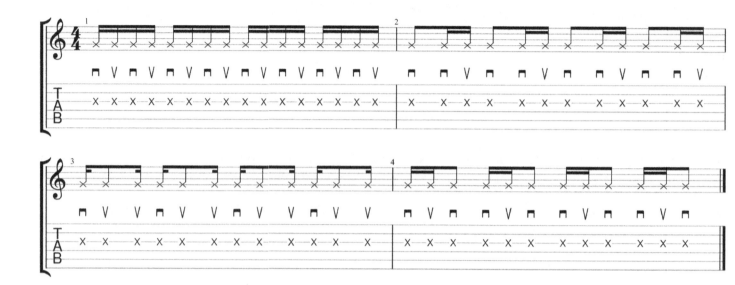

However, there are other 1/16th note groupings that can be created by incorporating 1/16th note rests into these patterns. Let's first study how the feel of the riff changes if we replace the 1/8th notes in the previous diagram with a 1/16th note followed by a 1/16th note rest.

In musical notation, a 1/16th note rest is written like this: ⅞

Begin by comparing the sound of an 1/8th note to that of a 1/16th note followed by a 1/16th note rest. Compare the notation in the first bar with the notation in the second.

This example uses an E5 power chord. Relax the pressure in your fretting hand to create the rests in bar two.

Example 4a:

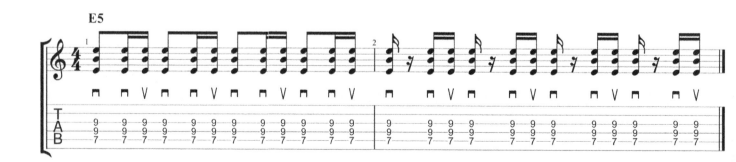

Now listen to and play the same phrase line with a fully muted strum instead of a power chord. Remember to mute and strum all of the strings, the single notes are written for clarity only.

As you can hear, both bars sound identical when played with muted strums.

Example 4b:

In Example 4a you heard that a 1/16th note followed by a 1/16th note rest creates a very different rhythmic effect than just using an 1/8th note. The second bar is more aggressive than the first, even though the actual accents of each rhythm are identical.

Try playing the remaining 1/16th note rhythmic combinations from the previous page in this way. Using an E5 chord, play the first bar using an 1/8th note and the second bar using a 1/16th note followed by a 1/16th note rest.

The only difference between each bar is that instead of letting the 1/8th notes ring, you are killing them by gently releasing the pressure with the fretting hand.

You don't need to hit all the strings every time. Try to let the guitar part breathe.

Example 4c:

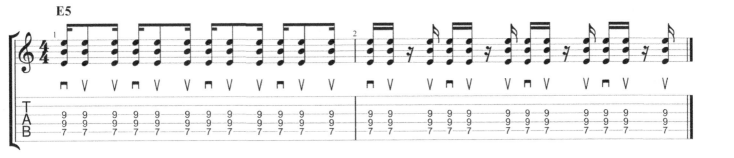

Example 4d:

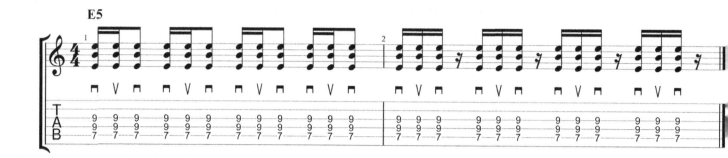

To highlight the difference between using a full 1/8th note and 1/16th note followed by a 1/16th note rest, you may wish to play these different groupings in quick succession.

Example 4e:

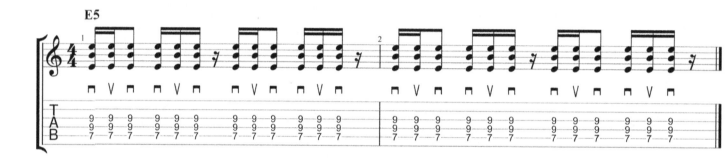

Make sure you can use this approach with all of the 1/16th note and 1/8th note combinations.

Now combine some of these combinations. Pay careful attention to the note lengths in each grouping. Control the muting in your fretting hand so that you clearly articulate the difference between an 1/8th note and a 1/16th note followed by a 1/16th note rest.

Example 4f:

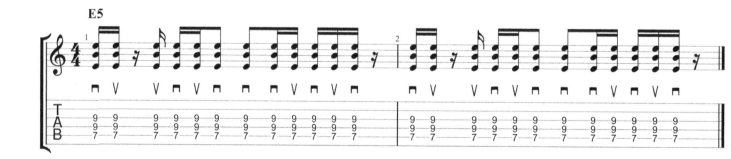

Example 4g:

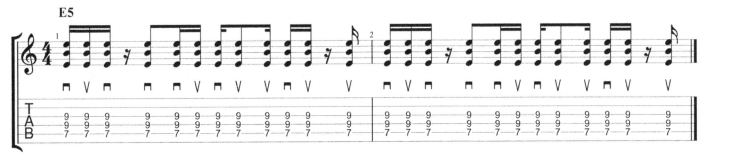

Example 4h:

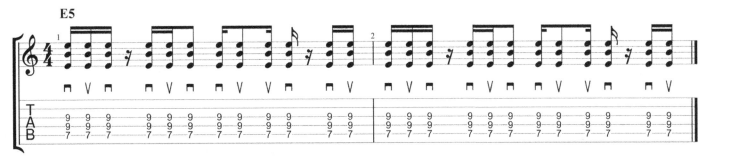

Invent and practice as many variations of this idea as you can think of. Once you have mastered these rhythms, try changing chords throughout each example to create interesting and original power chord riffs.

Further Groupings with 1/16th Note Rests

There is one important 1/16th note grouping that we have not yet considered: leaving a 1/16th note rest on the *first* beat of each bar.

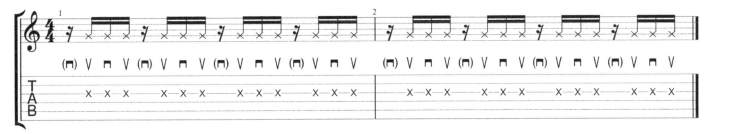

By placing a 1/16th note rest on the first division, a rhythmic 'hole' is created on the beat. This is an extremely effective musical idea.

Notice that the first down-strum is bracketed in each beat so it is not played. Don't forget that your strumming hand should never stop moving up and down. In order to leave the rest, simply *miss the strings* as you pass them on the first down-strum.

Once again, this rhythm is written on a single note for clarity. It is easier to begin by playing these examples with full muted strums across all the strings.

Missing the first 1/16th note of a beat is quite tricky at first. The easiest way to learn it is to play one full bar of muted 1/16th notes before switching to the altered rhythm in the next bar. This is shown in Example 4i.

The first bar will get your hand moving correctly, then in the second bar miss out the first *down* of every group of four.

Example 4i:

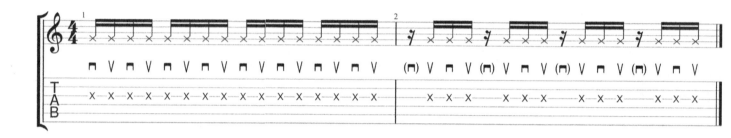

Start by playing this exercise at 60bpm and gradually increase the metronome speed to approximately 120 bpm. Try to feel your foot tapping in the 'hole' left by the missed strum.

When you have gained confidence with this rhythm, gradually incorporate it into your practice by using the following exercises.

Begin by playing each exercise with fully muted strums before playing the exercise on a single muted string, and then introducing an E5 chord. Finally, add a simple chord sequence to create an original riff. Keep these sequences simple to start with, but you can change chords wherever you like to create some very interesting phrases.

Example 4j:

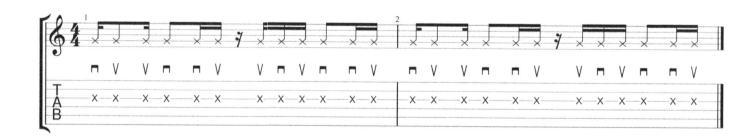

Example 4k:

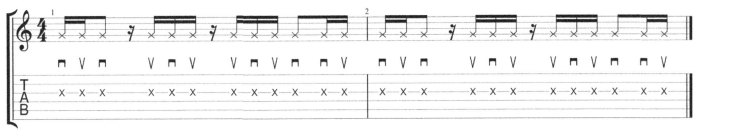

Example 4l:

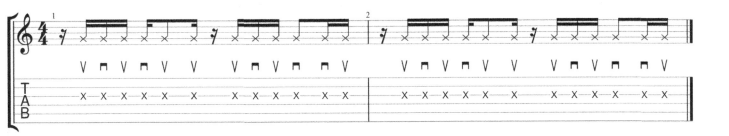

Come up with as many rhythmic variations as you can. Start slow and always focus on accuracy ahead of speed. Speed comes much more easily once you are in control of these patterns.

It is possible to add two, or even three 1/16th note rests into a four-note grouping to create rhythms which are even more syncopated.

Let's begin by adding two 1/16th note rests to the end of each grouping. On paper, this can be written in two different ways because two 1/16th note rests are equal to one 1/8th note rest.

Example 4m:

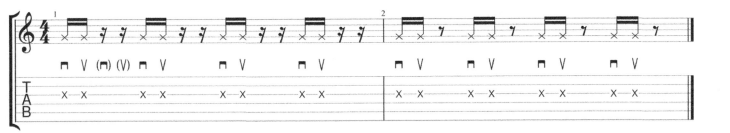

Don't forget to keep moving your strumming hand in time! Repeat the previous example but add in a simple E5 chord to create a hard rock riff. Try moving the power chord around to different locations. You could move up or down by two frets each time.

Use this new rhythmic grouping in some longer phrases. Here's one to get you started. Begin with fully muted strums, but quickly add power chords to create interesting rock riffs. Remember that you can change chord on any beat, or even between beats!

Example 4n:

The following example combines the above rhythm with the one taught in Example 4i:

Example 4o:

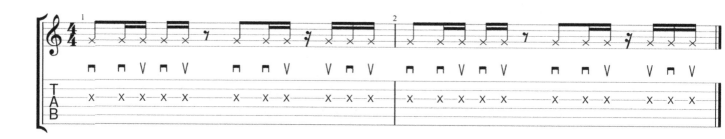

Repeat the previous few examples using power chords in place of the muted strums to create new riffs.

We will be going into much more detail about actual chords and riffs in the second part of this book, but to kick-start your creativity here is a rocky riff that uses the above rhythm.

Example 4p:

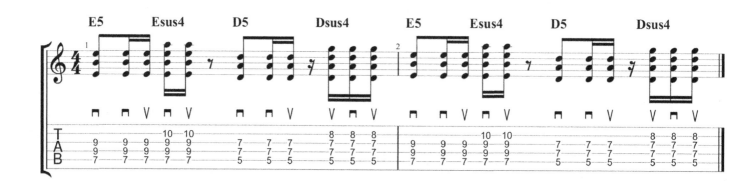

You can hear how simply adding a couple of chords can transform these rhythms into a Van Halen style rock groove. Try adding these chords to some of the previous examples.

The beauty of this kind of practice is that it opens your ears to many musical possibilities you may not have even conceived of before. You're learning rhythm, but you are also internalising new possibilities... Don't be afraid to get creative and simply play what you hear.

This chapter contains a great deal of information and will take a long time to absorb fully. There are also plenty more rhythm exercises in the Apprendix at the back of this book. Check them out when you get time, but don't forget to work on musical examples too.

Pick one or two rhythms each day and practice moving between them. Gradually build longer and longer phrases and focus on accuracy.

These rhythms underpin almost every aspect of rock guitar rhythm playing and it is essential to have them under your fingers.

Use a metronome and backing tracks to ensure that these rhythms are as tight and in the groove as possible.

Remember, the rhythmic permutations in this section are quite advanced. As I mentioned in the introduction, there is no need to work through this book sequentially – you can be learning chords and riffs from later chapters while also developing tight rhythm skills. Divide up your practice between these two disciplines.

Don't tackle Chapter Five, however, until you are very confident with everything that has gone before.

Chapter Five: Single Note Groupings

To further your rhythmic knowledge and freedom you should now learn to play groupings that contain only one 1/16th note.

Obviously, there are only four possible rhythms:

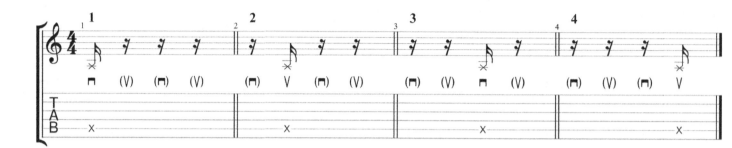

These single-note stabs frequently appear in progressive rock songs, but even if that isn't your cup of tea, learning this sparse rhythmic approach will dramatically improve your rhythmic placement.

As with any new musical concept, it is important to be very conscious and *cognitive* while you're learning, but very soon you will be able to play these rhythms unconsciously and musically. Ideally you don't want to be too cerebral (thought-out) when you play. In fact, you should try to switch off the 'inner monologue' side of your brain entirely. However, when you are learning something new, it is important to be as mentally involved as possible so you both understand and feel what you are playing.

To develop your control and placement of these single 1/16th notes, I would suggest playing one full bar of continuous 1/16th notes followed by one bar of your chosen rhythmic grouping. Remember that your strumming hand never stops moving up and down in 1/16th note divisions, so simply focus on making contact with the strings at the correct time.

Once again, use fully muted strums, even though the rhythm is notated in single notes. Move to single notes and chords as you gain confidence.

Here is the first rhythm:

Example 5a:

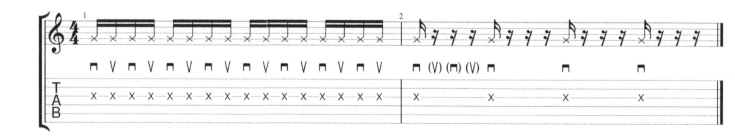

Example 5a should be very simple for you as the single, muted 1/16th note feels the same as playing a muted 1/4 note in bar two. Remember though, there is a difference between playing muted strums and full ringing chords. Try the previous example again, but this time using an E5 chord.

Make sure that the E5 chord is muted cleanly after each strum in bar two. It should sound like this:

Example 5b:

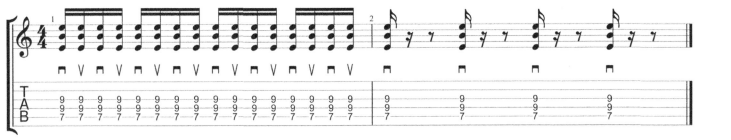

Now try combining both groupings into one bar.

Example 5c:

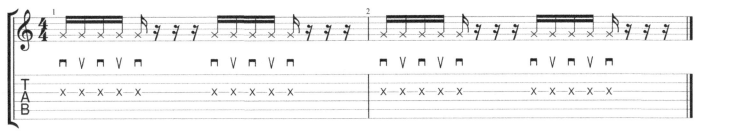

Then incorporate the rhythm into a full phrase.

Example 5d:

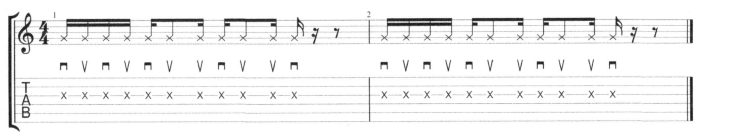

Try improvising some rhythms that use this single 1/16th fragment. Don't forget to play full chords too!

Now move on to the next rhythm. This particular grouping is one of the trickier ones to master as it is played with a single up-strum.

Use fully muted strums.

Example 5e:

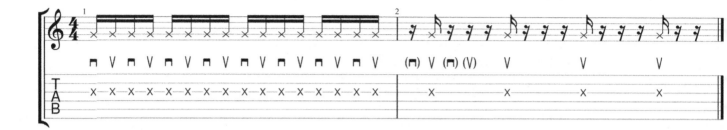

Combine the rhythms.

Example 5f:

Next, play the phrase with an E5 chord to check you can mute in the correct place.

Example 5g:

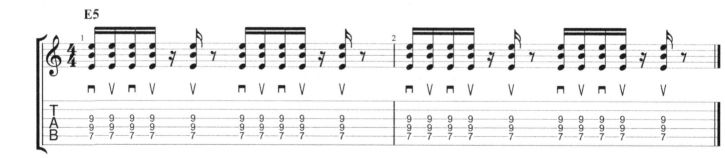

Finally, combine the new 1/16th note grouping with the ones you have already mastered before getting creative and experimenting with your own one-bar rhythms.

Example 5h:

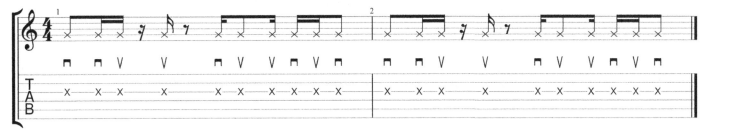

I'm sure you're getting the idea of how this process works, so to save space I will give you only the first exercise for rhythms three and four from page 27.

Example 5i:

Example 5j:

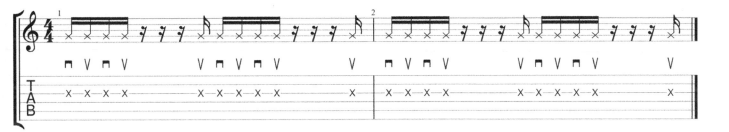

Work with these rhythms until you are extremely confident with them.

As you improve, you will soon begin to hear these ideas already fully formed in your head. This is when the exercises start becoming musical and your creative brain is engaged.

It is very important to listen to and transcribe rock guitar parts from records. The rhythmic and technical skills you have developed so far in this book will help you to hear and feel how a rock rhythm works. Try your hardest to 'lock in' with the guitar player on the record and emulate their *feel* as much as possible.

You will quickly find that these ideas naturally become part of your playing.

That is enough rhythm work for now, but I suggest that you keep returning back to this section to practice your skills. The next few chapters focus on how chords are commonly used in rock rhythm and look at some techniques that are used to inject energy and interest.

Part Two: Chords, Riffs and Music

Chapter Six: Rock Guitar Chords

Power Chords

In the rhythm chapters, we made great use of power chords. Power chords are probably the most commonly used chords in rock guitar and they have been played on thousands of songs in many different genres.

Power chords are popular in rock because not only do they have a heavy sound, they also do not contain the 'chord defining' 3rd interval, meaning that they are neither Major nor minor. As power chords only contain the root and the 5th of a chord they sound like a reinforced version of the root note.

So far, you have seen power chords played with roots on both the 6th string and the 5th string:

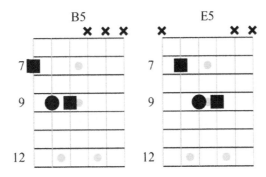

However, these chords can also be voiced on the top-string groups. Learn the following voicings:

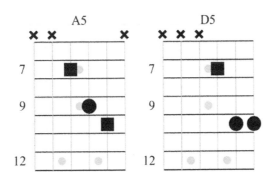

Be careful which strings you strum. Do not play any strings marked with an 'X'.

When playing faster rock songs, it is common to combine muting in both hands to keep unwanted strings quiet. For example, if you were playing the E5 chord shown above, you could gently rest your strumming hand on the low E (6th) string of the guitar to mute it with your palm.

When playing chords with a root on the 5th, 4th or 3rd string, it is also normal to allow the 1st finger of the fretting hand to 'overshoot' the root note of the chord and make gentle contact with the side of the unused string below. Muting the lower string with the fretting finger allows for slightly less accuracy in the strumming hand.

The high E and B (1st and 2nd) strings are normally muted naturally by the underside of your fretting hand fingers, but be careful not to apply too much pressure here so you don't create unwanted notes.

Play through the following exercise gradually increasing the tempo. Use a little gain on your amp to help you hear if you're using the correct muting.

Unused strings should be muted, and only the chord notes should ring.

Example 6a:

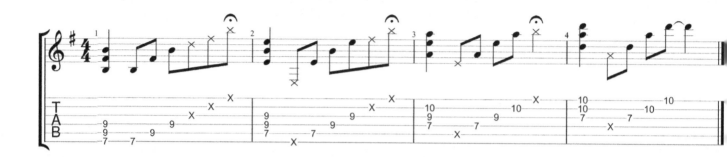

Although less common, there is another type of power chord that doubles the 5th of the chord and plays it in the bass to produce a thick, recognisable *inversion* of the power chord.

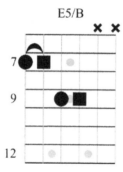

This chord voicing was used to great effect by one of the greatest guitarists of the last century. Check out the following example:

Example 6b:

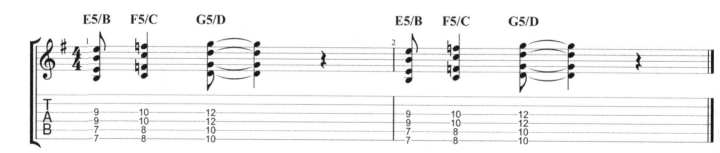

Splitting the Chord

A popular technique that creates texture is to 'split' the chord into two separate parts: the bass note and the actual chord notes, rather than strumming the whole chord at once. The technique is shown here with power chords, but you should try it with any of the chord ideas later in this section.

Play only the bass note of the chord on beats 1 and 3 and then fill in the rest of the chord on beats 2 and 4.

Example 6c:

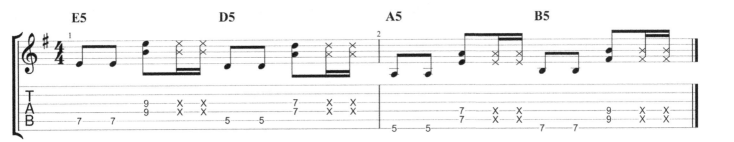

Notice the 'scratched', muted notes in the previous example that give more forward motion to the riff. To perform these scratches, continue to hold the chord but reduce the pressure with your fretting fingers so that they are just resting on the strings. When you pick the strings you should get a muted effect as heard in the audio example.

Rock guitarists are continually (and unconsciously) changing the pressure used in the fretting hand to shift between muted and full chords. This creates exciting dynamics and texture in the rhythm guitar part.

The chord splitting technique can be reversed by playing a full chord *on* the beat and filling in the rhythm with repeated bass notes.

Play the following example using all down strums.

Example 6d:

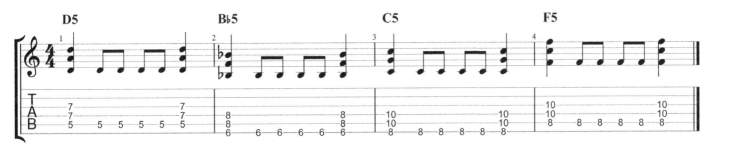

Another useful technique is to combine full strums with individually picked notes in each chord.

Example 6e:

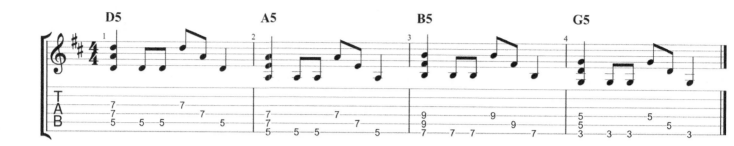

All these techniques can be combined to create rich, interesting musical textures. Notice the 'pushed' chord in the last beat of each bar pre-empts the chord change.

Example 6f:

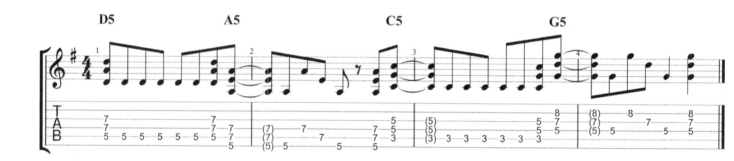

Power chords don't always have to be played as a three-note voicing with a doubled root note, in fact, they are often played with just the root and 5th. Compare the sound of the following two chords when played with high distortion:

Example 6g:

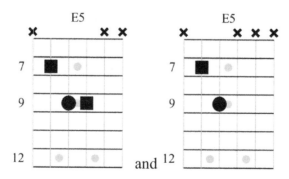

Playing with high gain or distortion actually adds to, and enhances the harmonic overtones or 'range' of the chord being played, so it can often be desirable to reduce the number of notes we play so as not to overpower the rest of the band.

The second, two-note voicing of the E5 power chord normally sounds more 'focused' than the first as it generates fewer harmonic overtones.

If you refer back to Example 6b, you will see that the root of a power chord does not have to be played in the bass.

Compare the following two voicings of C5.

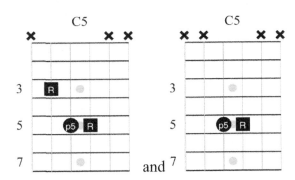

As you can see, the second chord is a two-note voicing of the C5 chord with the 5th in the bass. As simple as it may seem, this is one of the most important chord voicings in rock guitar because of the following type of riff:

Example 6h:

As you can hear, this type of power chord voicing has a crisp, articulate tone.

This power chord voicing can be shifted across onto the 5th and 4th strings for a deeper, more resonant tone. These mini voicings were popular with Mark Knopfler. Use your first finger throughout:

Example 6i:

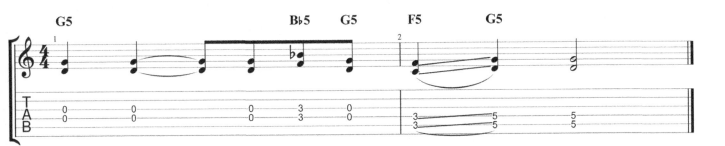

Two-note power chords played on the 4th and 3rd strings regularly occur in rock, and they're great fun to experiment with. Dial in some crunch and write a few of your own riffs using just these voicings.

Here are two to get you started:

Example 6j:

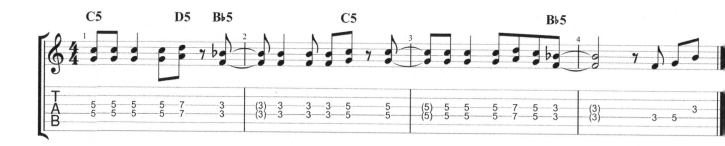

The final few notes of the previous example form a *fill* that both adds interest and helps the lick to loop more smoothly. Using lead lines in rhythm guitar parts will be discussed further in chapter eight.

Example 6k:

Finally, returning to the 'standard' power chord shape on page 42, there is another common movement that was popular in '80s rock, with players like Eddie Van Halen and Nuno Bettencourt all using this idea.

The technique is to stretch the first finger down a fret from the starting position, before returning to the original chord. Learn the following example with the two-note power chord shape as written, but then try re-fingering it to use the full, three-note power chord shape.

Example 6l:

Open-Position Chords

While open-position chords are often associated with acoustic guitar playing, they are also a regular part of many rock guitar riffs. In fact, the use of open chords in rock is a thread that runs from the early beginnings of rock in the '50s right through to the modern day.

It is strange today to think of musicians like Bill Haley, Cliff Richard, Buddy Holly and Ike Turner as cutting edge rock musicians, but in their day their music caused great controversy and public outrage while pushing the boundaries of popular music.

When playing open chords in rock we continually use slight note alterations or omissions to add interest, and make technical adjustments to keep them sounding tight and aggressive so they don't get overpowered by the amplifier's distortion.

While often used in isolation for rhythmic 'vamps', e.g., *Summer of '69* by Bryan Adams, often the beauty of open chords lies in the fact that they can easily be adjusted or embellished to form interesting riffs and melodies around simple chord shapes. This is the approach taken by many great guitarists from Buddy Holly to Brian May to Angus Young.

We will begin with some simple rhythmic vamping ideas before developing them further.

Many chord vamps fall into similar structures. Quite often you will see something that is two or four bars long with a small fill at the end leading back to the beginning of the riff. In the following example, notice how the sequence is 'pushed', right from the first bar.

I use the 'splitting the chord' technique from page 44 and combine it with tight palm muting to create a percussive effect. Notice how the strumming is limited to just a few strings to keep the riff tight and controlled.

Example 6m:

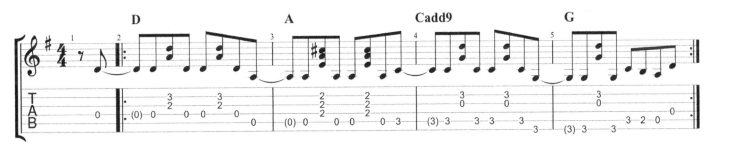

The next idea uses just three chords but adds a *rake* to decorate the first chord. A rake is performed like a slightly slower strum where the pick is dragged or 'raked' through the strings to articulate every note. Listen to the audio to hear how this technique should sound.

Hold down the chord shown in each chord symbol, each melody note of the riff is contained in the held chord.

Example 6n:

Hold down each chord...

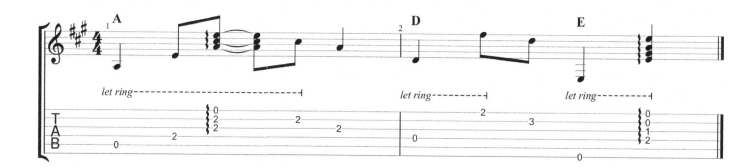

The previous example was based on the style of Buddy Holly, but here is the same chord sequence with more of a punk/rock approach.

Example 6o:

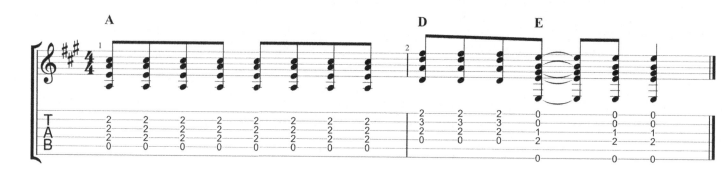

The previous two examples show a contrasting use of the same chord progression, and teaches us a valuable lesson: in rock music there are many identical chord sequences, it's how they are played that defines the feel of the music.

The following example is one of the most frequently heard rhythms in rock guitar playing. It is common in the music of Guns N' Roses and many other hard rock bands. To play the muted scratches, relax the pressure of your fretting hand and add slight palm muting. I suggest that you use down-strums for every 1/8th note.

Example 6p:

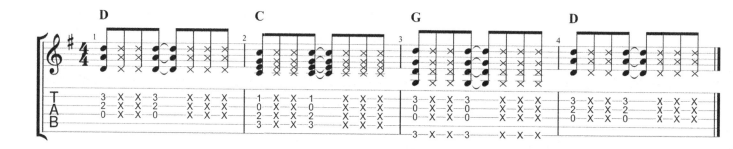

The earliest rock n' roll riffs grew out of the blues, and this influence has remained a continuous driving force in the development of rock. Many of these blues vamps have become rock staples and are often based around a single chord with variations and fills played in the bass. These ideas are often played in the 'open keys' of A, E and D Major.

The following riff idea is based in the key of A, but you could easily shift it into the key of E by moving the first chord down a string. Use your 1st finger to barre the open A chord.

Example 6q:

The following example is a standard rock rhythm idea that has been used by hundreds of artists, from the Rolling Stones to Status Quo. It is a variation of the previous idea, but incorporates more of a Texas-Blues style approach into the riff.

Notice that even though most of the voicings of the chords are just two-note selections of the bigger A and D Major chords, each chord can still be split into lower and upper sections. The bass notes are used to keep a 'chugging' rhythm feel and the higher notes of the chord are used to accent the chord in the riff.

You can keep this riff muted for a tight, percussive effect, or let the strings ring a little more for a more open, richer sound. Often both of these techniques will be used: tight and percussive in the verse and then open and ringing in the chorus to add energy and texture.

Any bluesy decorations to these chords are played using the spare fingers of the fretting hand.

Example 6r:

The ideas in the two previous examples can easily be combined and there are many possible ways to introduce new chords and fills. Listen carefully to your favourite rock bands and you will hear these ideas occurring frequently.

For more blues guitar riffs check out **The Complete Guide to Playing Blues Guitar: Rhythm Guitar.**

AC/DC are masters of using simple open chords to create anthemic rock guitar riffs. By combining split, muted and ringing chords they have managed to make some of the most memorable riffs of the past forty years.

Here's an idea in a classic rock style.

Example 6s:

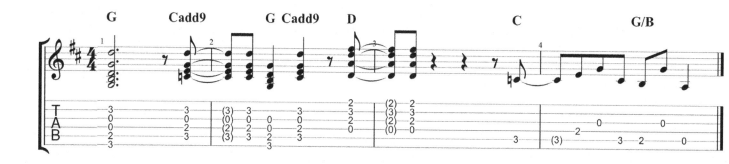

As always, listen to the audio example to get the right feel for this example. Notice how full strums are combined with smaller strums and single-string fills.

Here's another example in a similar style.

Example 6t:

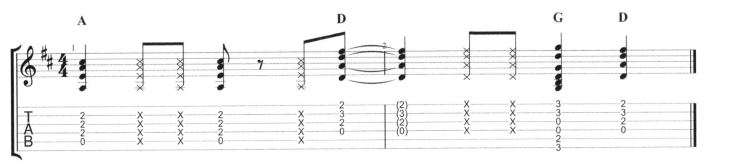

The previous example makes more use of right-hand mutes. Keep each A Major chord tight and percussive and let the D and G chords ring out.

As there are a fairly limited number of open-position chords used in classic rock riffs, often it's only the rhythm of the progression that makes a chord sequence easily identifiable.

The following two examples demonstrate the same chord progression played in two different ways. The first is as a classic punk riff, and the second is an iconic '90s pop/rock song.

Example 6u:

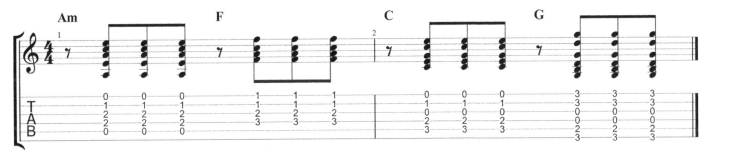

Example 6v:

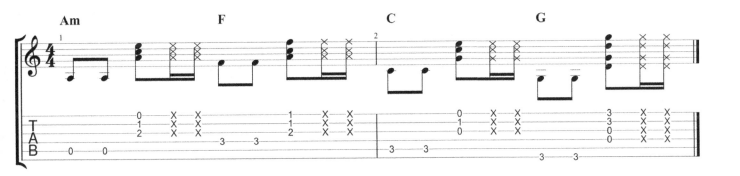

Open-position chords are a defining feature of many rock songs, and you will often see identical chord progressions used in different ways. Often for guitarists, songs are differentiated only by a particular rhythmic idea, tempo or lead guitar riff.

Listen analytically to as many rock songs as you can in the style that you want to learn. Try to transcribe the chord sequences by listening to the bassline, or find a transcription online. Make a note of the chords and pay attention to what makes that rhythm guitar part unique. Are the chords being held, muted, or is a combination of these techniques being used? Are there any muted scratches between chords and which chords are being accented?

Pay attention to what (if anything) is happening under a lead guitar riff or vocal part, and try to notice how the instruments complement each other. How many guitars can you hear? Is the rhythm guitar playing at the same time as the vocal or providing fills between each phrase?

Try to develop a 'dictionary' of rhythmic ideas and experiment as much as you can. Listen out for *embellishments* to open chords. Many common embellishments will be taught in the next chapter.

The best thing you can do as a musician is to listen to, and transcribe the music you like. It can be difficult at first so use online videos and tabs to help you, although the more you do by yourself the quicker you will learn.

Transcribing and learning music in this way will also help you to develop a repertoire of songs. Guitarists are notorious for learning only the famous riffs from popular tunes. If you set yourself apart by learning songs the whole way through, you should never be short of work.

So far we have looked at how basic open chords can be used, but there are many useful embellishments that can be made to each chord shape. We will look at these in the following chapter.

Chapter Seven: Embellishments

When playing open chords in rock guitar, it is normally very easy to add or remove a finger to create a very different sound. Tiny embellishments have often been used to create catchy guitar riffs.

For example, this riff uses simple variations to a D Major and A Major chord to create a memorable hook:

Example 7a:

This idea can also be used to create a country feel with the D chord.

Example 7b:

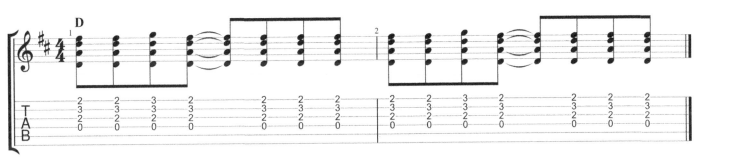

Every open chord always has many embellishments available, and we will study the most important ones here.

To clearly demonstrate the notes available I have notated these embellishments on chord grids. The original chord shape is in black and the possible additions are shown with a hollow circle. Sometimes two notes can be altered at the same time.

In addition, I have written a short riff for each chord that uses some of the available alterations, but you should spend as much time as you can getting creative with these ideas.

There isn't enough room to cover all the open chords used in rock guitar here, but I've tried to cover the most common uses. Always experiment with new chords to see where you can add or subtract a finger or two from the basic chord shape.

D Major

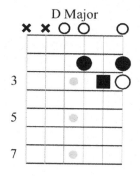

Example 7c:

A Major

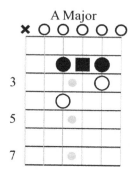

Example 7d:

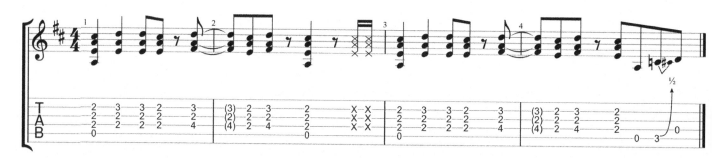

Also experiment by hammering on from the open strings notated in the chord diagram.

The double hammer-on in the above example is a very common movement and regularly occurs in the guitar parts of Brian May and Keith Richards. This shape is technically a barre chord voicing of a D/F# chord and will be addressed on page 71, but for now check out this riff that slides the barre chord up by two frets.

Example 7e:

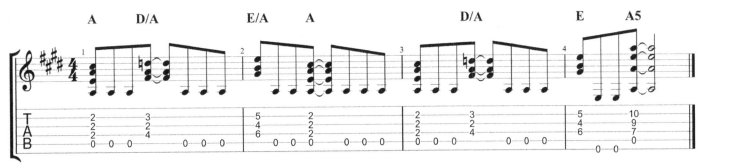

Often minor chords allow the same embellishments as Major chords. For example, the chord of A minor has many of the same embellishments as A Major.

A Minor

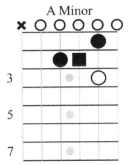

Example 7f:

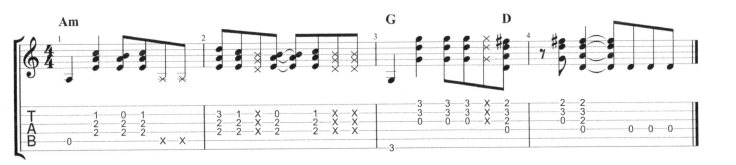

There are many possible embellishments available to all types of 'A' chords. The key is to experiment and listen to music in your chosen genre. Also, make sure that you check out music in styles that you may not normally listen to. For example, many folk progressions are easily adapted to the rock style.

F Major

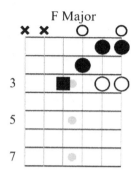

Example 7g:

The riff above is reminiscent of more modern 'Indie' bands like Franz Ferdinand and The Black Keys. Keep the riff tight and staccato by using your picking hand to chop down on the strings after each chord.

C Major

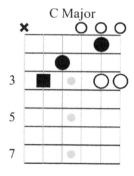

Example 7h:

The C Major idea above is a little folkier, but with the right tone and attitude it wouldn't be out of place in a Lynyrd Skynyrd track.

G Major

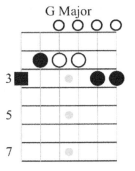

Example 7i:

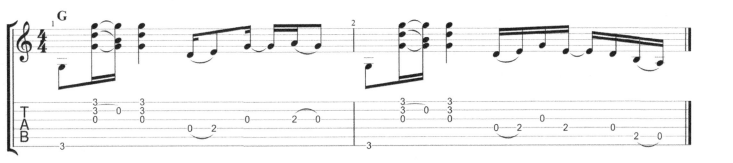

This riff is based on a typical '70s style rhythm.

E Minor

E minor is a key often used in heavy rock. Depending on the kind of mood you want to create, the embellishments may often change.

As always, experimentation is the way to create interesting rhythm guitar parts.

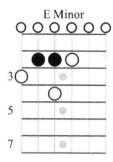

Example 7j:

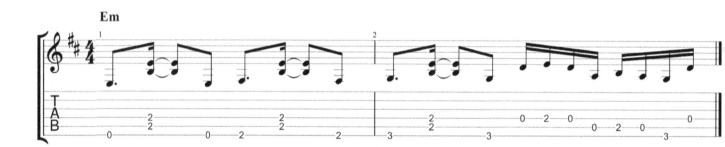

Every open chord can be altered and embellished in some way, and I would quickly fill this book if I went into great detail for every common chord. Spend time exploring each chord individually, and then combine some of the ideas to form interesting and melodic rhythmic ideas.

Often, similar simple ideas, such as the one below, work well over every chord in a progression.

Example 7k:

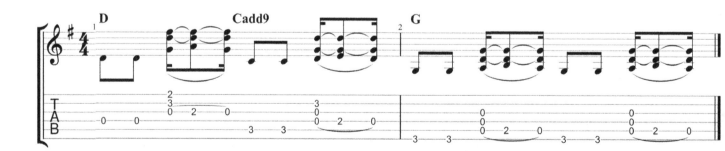

Generally, decorations to open chords occur in the main body of the chord (higher notes) and the root note is unaffected, but there are some important root note movements that you should know.

In rock (and acoustic) music, it is common to use a technique called a *descending bass* to link chords together. This will be examined in the next section.

Descending Basslines

Descending basslines have been used since the times of early baroque music but are now an integral part of rock rhythm guitar playing. They're great when used in an unaccompanied guitar part, but they also allow us to 'lock in' musically with the bass guitar to form a strong foundation for a song.

Check out the start of *Stairway to Heaven*, or the cool, sleazy descending basslines on Led Zeppelin's *Dazed and Confused*. For a more modern use, *Whatever* by Oasis makes a feature of the descending bassline on the acoustic guitar.

Without getting too technical, a descending bassline will normally join two chords together by adding a single note between each one. With open chords there are three important movements that you should know:

The first is the bass note moving down by step from G to Em:

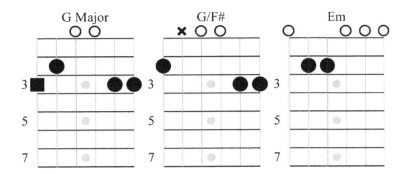

Example 71:

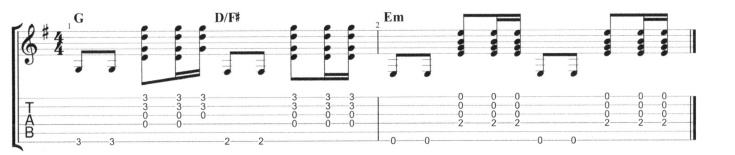

The next example shows the bass note moving down by step from C to A minor:

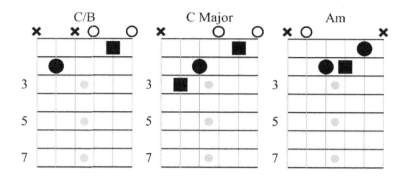

Example 7m:

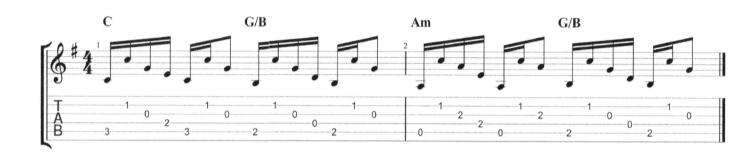

The final example is a bassline run-down from F Major to Dm7:

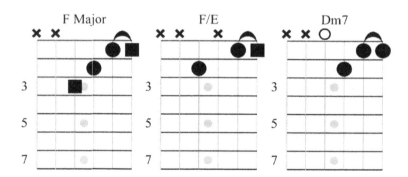

Example 7n:

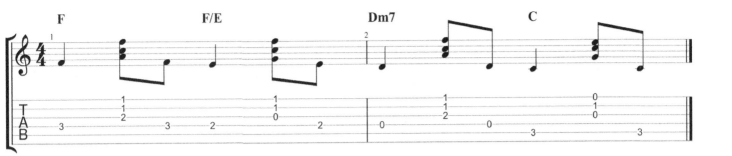

All these movements can be reversed to form an ascending bassline.

Now we have looked at the three main movements in descending basslines on open chords, let's combine some of these ideas to make a longer phrase. Jack Johnson uses a similar idea on *Better Together*, but here is the same sequence in a rock guitar setting.

Be careful with the Bb barre chord in bar three, it can be a bit tricky at first. If you are struggling, try changing the position of your thumb on the neck.

Example 7o:

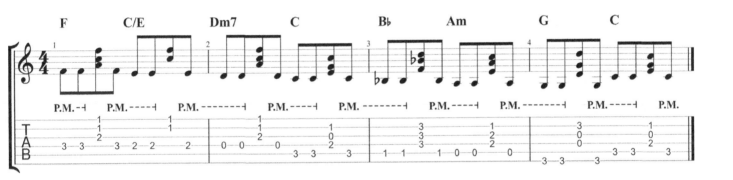

The next example is a little folky, but it would make a great intro to a heavier rock song or a quieter middle section in a ballad.

In this example, I combine some of the embellishments from earlier to create an *ascending* melody while the bassline descends as before. For more of this kind of approach, check out Nick Cave, John Martyn or even Joe Perry in a quieter moment.

Example 7p:

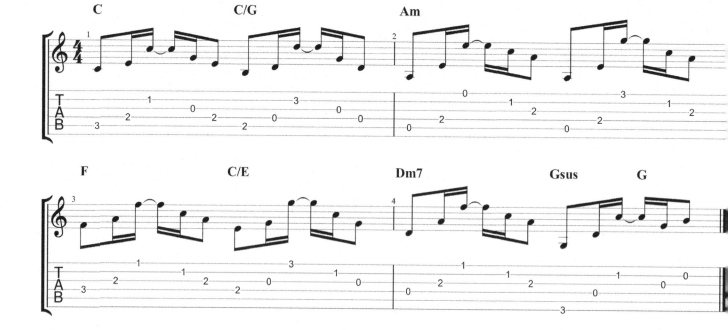

Descending basslines can also be used with power chords.

Example 7q:

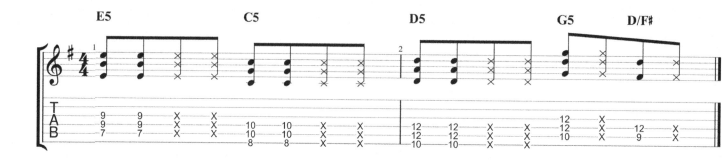

A great deal of rock songs use power chords so their mastery is essential if you want to become a fluent rhythm guitar player. Practice sliding long distances up and down the neck holding a power chord shape and also moving across adjacent strings so that you will be familiar with whatever future songs may throw at you.

Chapter Eight: Barre Chords and Single Lines

Open chords on the guitar are formed by playing a set pattern of notes and some of these notes are on the open strings. If we were to slide our fingers up the guitar, we change some of the notes in the chord, but the notes on the open strings wouldn't change. This means that we would no longer be playing a 'recognised' chord.

We can, however, use open chord shapes further up the neck if we find a way to take the notes on the open strings with us and retain the set pattern of notes. To do this, guitarists use *barre* chords to 'take the open strings with us' and keep the chord shapes the same.

The word barre comes from the Spanish word 'to bar' and normally the first finger is used to bar across the strings. We normally have to re-finger the chord shape slightly, but as there are no open strings, a barre chord can be played anywhere up and down a string.

For example, look at the following chord grids for the chord of Em:

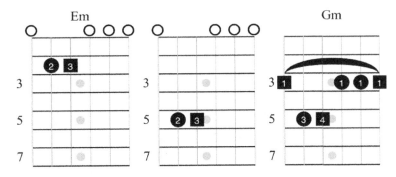

The first chord grid shows the chord of E minor (Em). Think of it as just a minor chord shape for now. This chord has a particular shape that includes some open strings.

If we move the chord up by three frets but allow the open strings to ring, we have changed the relationship between each of the notes and are no longer playing a minor chord.

However, if we replace the open strings in the second diagram with a barre across the third fret, then we have restored the relationship between the notes as seen in the original Em chord. The root of the chord is still on the sixth string, but now the root is on the third fret so the chord is *G minor*.

This barre chord is now a completely movable 'minor' shape. As long as you know the names of the notes on the sixth string, you can move this shape anywhere to form any minor chord.

For example, here are the barre chords of Am and Cm:

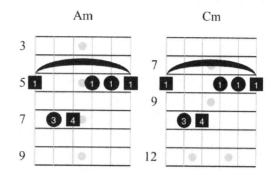

Learn the notes on the sixth string of the guitar and practice moving the barre chord around, saying the name of the chord out loud as you do so. Here are the notes on the sixth string:

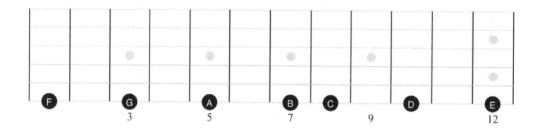

This process works for any chord. This minor chord shape has a root on the fifth string:

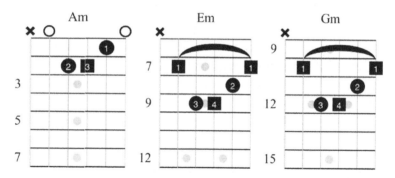

Learn the notes on the fifth string and once again practice moving this minor chord to different root notes. Say the name of each chord out loud each time.

As I'm sure you can tell, the big advantage of barre chords is that we only need to know one shape to play many different chords. We can move the same chord shape up and down the neck to access Gm, Am, and Bm, etc.

Sometimes it is very difficult to play certain open chords, so if you don't know how to play F#m as an open chord, you can just find the note F# on the sixth string (or the fifth string) and play the appropriate chord shape. This strategy is very useful for finding a way to play a chord shape you don't know.

Normally you don't want to move too far up and down one string because it will affect the tone of the chords so it is better to move across the strings if you can. For example, it would be better to play the chord sequence Gm to Cm as in the following diagram rather than playing them on the same string:

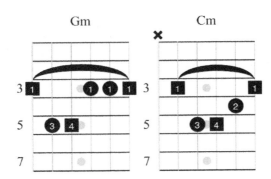

However, playing barre chords all on the same string does happen occasionally to create certain special effects.

There are three initial chord types you should know as barre chords. They are all constructed from open-position chord shapes. We have already looked at minor chord shapes, now learn the shapes for the Major and '7' chords with roots on the sixth and fifth strings.

Major Shapes:

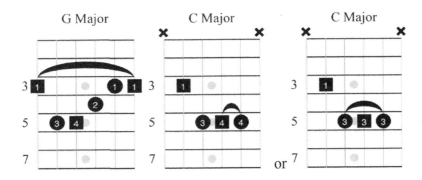

(Notice that the barre in the fifth string Major shape is played with the 4th finger which can be tricky. You could also use your 3rd finger to barre all three notes if you find it easier).

Dominant 7 or '7' shapes.

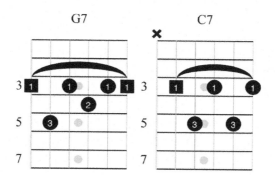

There are many other barre chord shapes, but once again these would completely fill this book. You will come across more shapes as you learn more songs, but if you're interested in developing your chord knowledge, check out my book **Guitar Chords in Context**.

Barre chords are tricky to learn at first and you will often find that you are muting notes or causing certain strings to buzz. Everyone struggles at first and my best advice is to practice in short bursts and continually try to adjust the position of your wrist and thumb if you are getting buzzes.

Make sure you take plenty of breaks and remain aware of the amount of pressure you're using.

Barre chords are often used in their full form to play simple chord progressions. One of the most famous progressions in rock can be played by holding down some of the chord shapes shown above.

Example 8a:

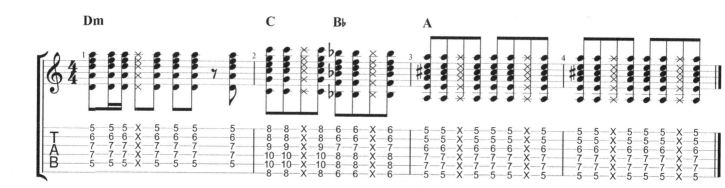

A great use of barre chords can be seen in this longer rock progression inspired by baroque music.

Example 8b:

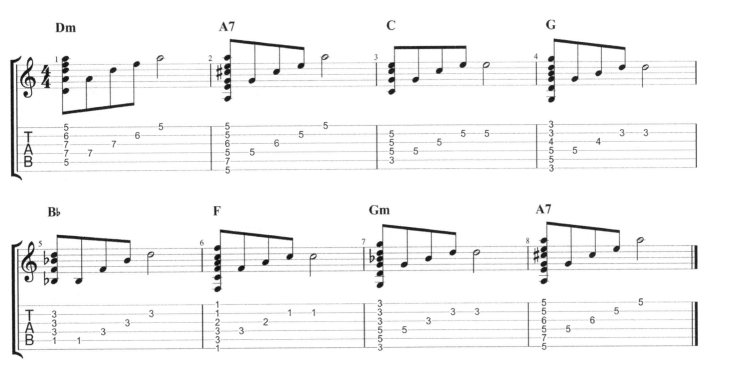

It can sometimes be appropriate to use barre chords with roots on the same string to create a specific effect.

Example 8c:

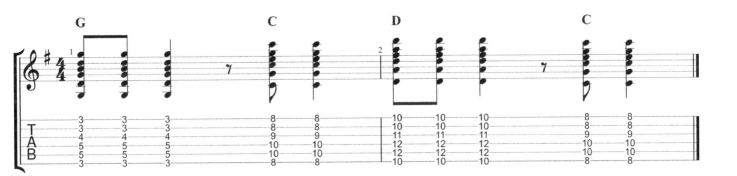

These chords can also be combined with the bluesy bass techniques shown in Chapter Seven. By splitting the chord and adding some bass movement it is possible to create an intricate guitar part typical of early rock songs.

Example 8d:

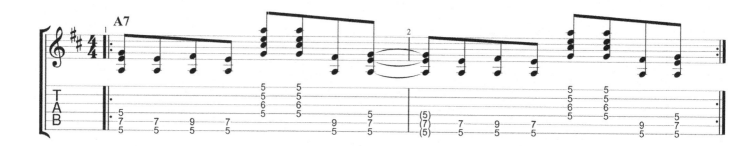

Full barre chords take up a lot of sonic 'space' in a band. We are covering a lot of frequencies that will probably be doubled by other musicians, especially if we're playing with a keyboard player. Even the lower note of the guitar can clash with the bass player if they are playing fills higher on the neck.

It is normally desirable to stay out of the way of the other instrumentalists in the band so often guitarists will limit their chord playing to just the top three or four strings on the guitar. There are two ways to do this, by either holding down the full barre chord and avoiding striking the bass notes with the pick, or by re-fingering the chord.

Both methods have different advantages, although re-fingering the chord leaves spare fingers that can embellish the rhythm part, as you saw earlier with open chords.

Major and minor barre chords are often re-fingered in the following ways.

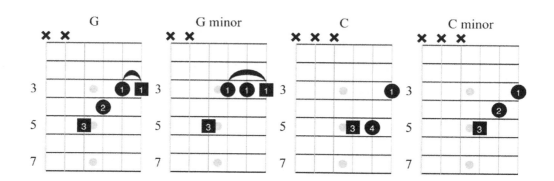

These partial barres are very useful and were frequently used in the early beginnings of rock music in the '50s and '60s.

Example 8e:

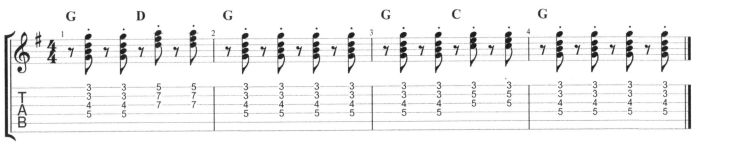

As not all the fingers are being used, this allows room for certain embellishments to be added.

Example 8f:

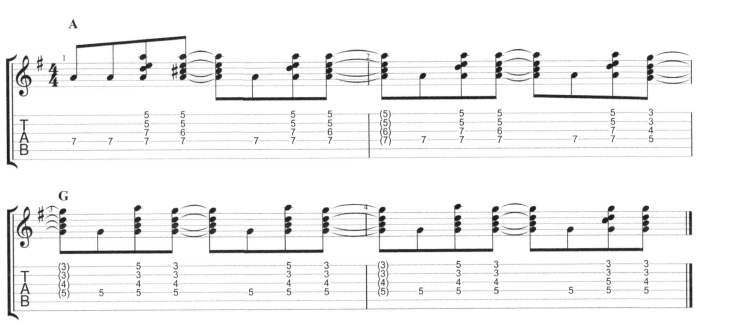

Jimi Hendrix took this idea one step further and hooked his thumb over the neck of the guitar to play a lower bass note of the chord on the sixth string.

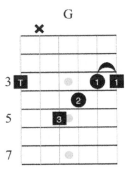

Jimi grew up playing in R&B bands in the '50s, so it is unsurprising he played rhythmic phrases like this.

Example 8g:

While we are on the subject of Jimi Hendrix, there is one barre chord that no rock guitar player can be without. The chord is a jazzy E7#9, but it's normally just called 'The Hendrix Chord'.

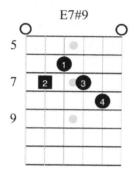

When this chord is played with a root note of E, it is common to use the open sixth string (E) as a doubled bass note.

The Hendrix chord has a very distinctive sound and once you can play it, it will always jump out at you when you hear it.

The following example teaches you a classic use of the 7#9 chord in rock guitar.

Example 8h:

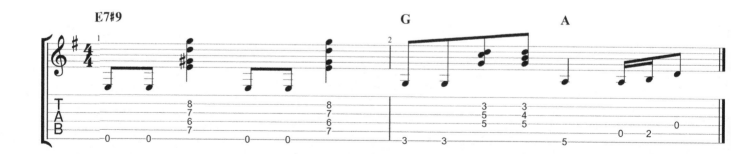

As with open chords, there are many embellishments available for each barre chord shape and I strongly encourage you to explore different fingerings and experiment with other notes if the chord shape allows it.

Earlier, we touched on an embellishment to an open A Major chord that can also be seen as a barre chord idea. Study the following diagrams:

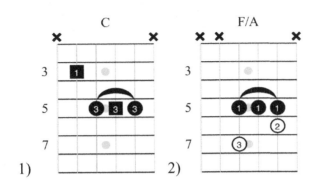

The first diagram shows a normal C Major barre chord and the second diagram shows the same chord re-fingered without the root note and with two embellishments added.

Barre the notes in the second diagram at the 5th fret and play the following simple line.

Example 8i:

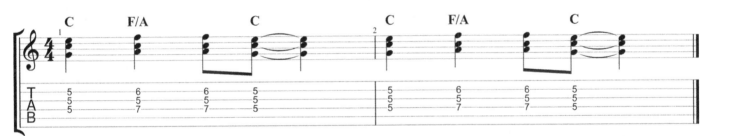

The C chord is played rootless and the F chord has its 3rd (A) in the bass.

C to F (chord I to chord IV) is probably the most common chord movement in music, but disguising it in this way helps it to sound fresh and new.

This chord movement occurs in hundreds of classic rock songs (although often in different keys with very different rhythms).

Check out the following examples:

Example 8j:

Example 8k:

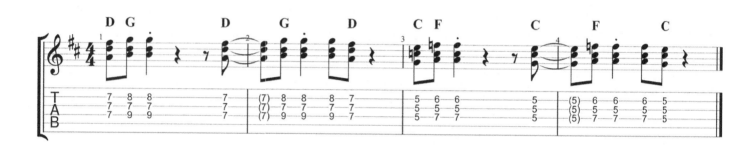

Example 8l:

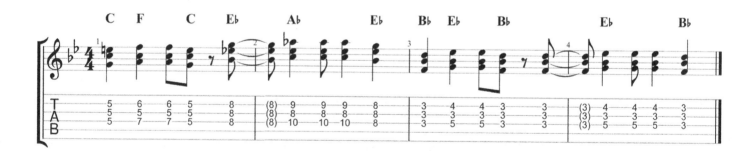

As you can hear, this combination of chords is extremely versatile and forms quite a large part of classic rock's rhythmic vocabulary.

Single Line Rhythm Playing

While chords and embellishments form a large part of rock guitar rhythm playing, many songs are built around single-note rhythmic ideas.

Often, these single-note lines are created by picking through individual chord shapes, but occasionally the single note phrase is the driving force behind the song.

These phrases are normally based on just a few notes of the minor pentatonic scale and use a lot of repetition so that the listener isn't too distracted from the singer's melody. Also, you will often find that the rhythms used in single note riffs are quite syncopated (played between the beats) so that they contrast with the placement of the vocal melody. This is shown in Example 8m:

Example 8m:

Example 8n:

This next riff leaves lots of room for other instruments, such as a synth and a Hammond organ.

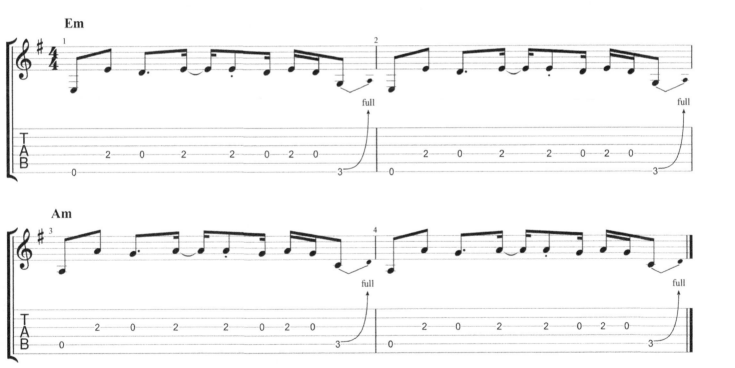

Sometimes all you need is a descending scale and a pedal bass note.

Example 8o:

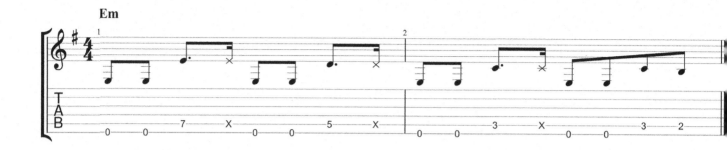

Jimi Hendrix was a master of using just a few notes to lay down a whole song's rhythm part.

Example 8p:

It really is true that less is often more. If you're playing in a band with other instruments, then you might only need a short repeating sequence of notes to add a bit of movement and colour to a track. If there is another guitar in the band, it is rare that you would want both guitars playing exactly the same part.

Classic Rock Style File

The final part of this book looks at some classic rock rhythm ideas from the past six decades. Of course, the music across any ten-year period will be varied and diverse, but certain stylistic elements do tend to stand out.

Starting from the beginnings of rock in the '50s we will examine rhythm figures that have become essential knowledge for the modern guitarist.

You will see how the vocabulary covered so far in this book can be brought together to form some innovative and ground breaking music.

If you're only into modern music, don't discount ideas that you feel are 'dated' and old fashioned. Music has a timeline and a history, and all new music builds in some way on the vocabulary of the past. Music also comes in and out of fashion. Famous rock bands of the '90s were heavily influenced by the music of the '60s, and '80s shred rock came back for a time in the early '00s.

All rock guitarists are in some way influenced and indebted to the musicians who went before, and understanding the influences of your guitar heroes will help you to develop a deep knowledge of your icon's style.

For example, Jimmy Page was heavily influenced by the early blues guitarists and grew up playing Skiffle.

Eric Clapton was heavily influenced by Muddy Waters and Robert Johnson. Eddie Van Halen cited Eric Clapton as an essential influence.

Tony Iommi said that Django Reinhardt and Hank Marvin were important players in his development as a musician. The family tree of rock gets quite complicated!

It just goes to show that you never know how a legend's playing has developed. My advice is to listen to everything you can and learn to analyse a song, even if it's 70 years old. Figure out what makes it work and write riffs using those approaches.

Before you know it, you'll have a catalogue of riffs in many different styles and you'll be on your way to becoming a creative songwriter.

As I mentioned in the introduction, I can't give exact, note for note transcriptions of pieces here, as it would be an intellectual copyright violation. This section contains riffs *in the style of* important bands from each decade.

Warning! The following sections contain extensive recommended listening lists. Your favourite albums may not be listed, but I assure you this is for reasons of limited space rather than a deliberate omission. Feel free to get in touch via **www.fundamental-changes.com** if you feel I've missed anything obviously genre-defining!

Chapter Nine: Rock Rhythm Guitar through the Decades

The 1950s

The 1950s saw the first beginnings of rock fuelled in part by the introduction of the first commercially available solid body electric guitar in 1948. It is widely considered that the first rock n' roll song was *Rocket 88* by Ike Turner, featuring a distorted guitar part based on the jive and rhythm and blues of the '30s and '40s. Throughout the decade, rock n' roll began to evolve with other notable artists including Bill Haley and his Comets, Fats Domino, Chuck Berry, Little Richard, Eddie Cochran Buddy Holly and, of course, Elvis Presley.

While the electric guitar was becoming more common in popular music, much of 1950s rock n' roll is driven by the piano. Don't discount artists like Fats Domino whose music was predominantly piano driven.

Recommended Listening

Chuck Berry is on Top – Chuck Berry

Rock and Roll – Elvis Presley

The "Chirping" Crickets – The Crickets

Here's Little Richard – Little Richard

Go Bo Diddley – Bo Diddley

Buddy Holly – Buddy Holly

Shake, Rattle and Roll – Bill Haley and his Comets

Jailhouse Rock – Elvis Presley

Rhythm Styles

As early Rock n' Roll grew out of R&B it's not surprising to find a great deal of its influence in this first decade. In the style of Bill Haley, this guitar part leaves a gap on beat one (as was common in the guitar parts of most R&B) and also uses a rich E9 chord in the third bar.

Example 9a:

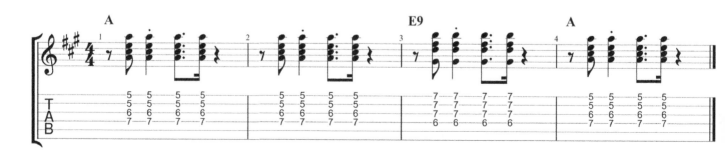

Early rock guitar also borrowed heavily from blues and R&B chord progressions, although instead of a lazy triplet feel, rock was often up-tempo and even.

The following example in the style of Chuck Berry is a common chord structure in rock. It's based on the chord sequence of a standard 12 bar blues, but everything is compressed into just 8 bars. The 8 bar blues became a staple of rock guitar and has been commonly used over the last sixty years, with bands like Status Quo making a whole career out of this type of idea.

In this example, use your first and third fingers to play the initial power chord and reach out with your 4th finger to hit the 9th fret. If you can't quite reach, try dropping your thumb down the neck a bit. Experiment with different amounts of palm muting in the picking hand.

Example 9b:

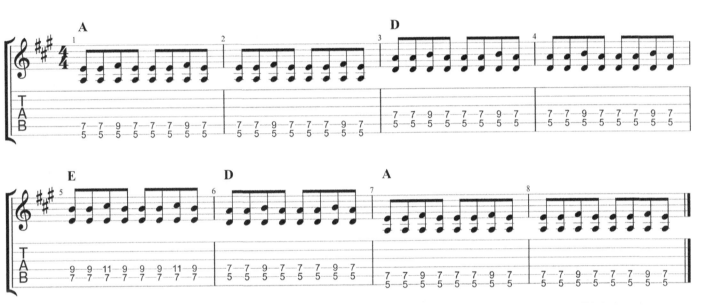

Rhythm guitarists would also play single note 'bass style' arpeggio lines that allowed plenty of room for a piano to play an improvised chord part. Often this part would be played with distortion to cut through the other instruments.

Try playing the following single note line around the chord changes in any of the previous examples. Outlining chords with arpeggio ideas can be a great contrast to another guitar part that is playing simple chords.

Example 9c:

The rock n' roll music of the '50s was the founding bedrock of everything that would come afterwards. It is important to know the roots of the style you want to play, and these sorts of riffs come in extremely handy for a day-to-day working musician.

The genre-defining music of the '60s took many of the features of 1950s rock n' roll and melded them into a raw and powerful form.

The 1960s

The 1960s was the decade where rock music came into its own and diversified greatly. While musicians like Elvis were still having regular chart success, the 'British invasion' of The Rolling Stones, Cream, The Who and Led Zeppelin, amongst many others were making names for themselves. The '60s started to see more of a cross-pollination of music across the Atlantic, with US artists like Jimi Hendrix and The Velvet Underground appearing in the UK Charts.

The lyrical content of rock music started to move towards political commentary and social awareness highlighted by The Who's *My Generation*. It is interesting to note, however, that a lot of the tracks on the album of the same name still owe a lot to R&B and blues.

In the US, rock music started to get prime-time coverage on programmes like the Ed Sullivan Show, and the late '60s saw the first rock festivals, culminating in 1969 when half a million people went to the three-day Woodstock festival.

Recommended Listening

My Generation – The Who

Are you Experienced / Electric Ladyland / Axis: Bold as Love – Jimi Hendrix

Disraeli Gears / Goodbye – Cream

The Animals – The Animals

Kinks – The Kinks

Sgt Pepper's Lonely Hearts Club Band / A Hard Day's Night / The White Album – The Beatles

Led Zeppelin / Led Zeppelin 2 – Led Zeppelin

The Doors – The Doors

The Rolling Stones / Aftermath / Let it Bleed / Between the Buttons – The Rolling Stones

The Band – The Band

The Velvet Underground – The Velvet Underground and Nico

Green River – Creedence Clearwater Revival

Roger the Engineer / Little Games / For Your Love – The Yardbirds

In the Court of the Crimson King – King Crimson

Black Sabbath – Black Sabbath

It is impossible to list all of the important musicians and bands of the 1960s here, so extensive listening is required! The whole Beatles back catalogue is essential listening, as is the work of Hendrix, The Rolling Stones, Cream and Led Zeppelin. It is also important to check out the bands signed to Motown records, and the re-emergence of African American artists via the Atlantic and Stax Record Labels. Music doesn't exist in a vacuum and a wide depth of listening is needed to hear how the styles influenced each other.

Rhythm Styles

The first example shows just one way bands in the 1960s built on the 'standard' chord I to IV progression. By using power chords approaching the target chord from a tone below they could create a dynamic, hard-hitting riff.

Example 9d:

The next example shows how a simple folky chord progression can be given the 1960s rock treatment. While many bands were throwing out power chords, these four chords formed one of the biggest selling and most enduring songs of the 60s.

This example can be played clean and allowed to ring out, but also try adding some gain and tightening up the muting and playing the part straight, not swung as it is written.

It just goes to show that sometimes all you need is four chords and some great lyrics.

Example 9e:

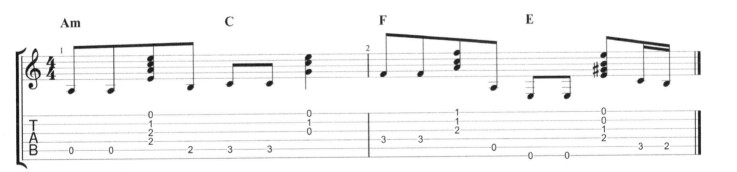

A rhythm guitar part can also be driven by a single line phrase, with artists like the Rolling Stones, Jimi Hendrix, and Led Zeppelin all using this approach. Often it's the catchiness of this hook that makes the song instantly recognisable.

Use enough fuzz to get your guitar to start breaking up and add some phasing to create a 60s vibe.

Example 9f:

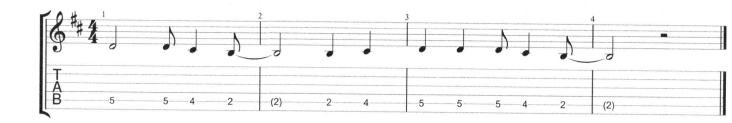

The next example shows a great way to combine a lead line with a devastating power chord riff.

Turn it up loud and keep the strumming tight.

Example 9g:

Some would argue that the '60s culminated with the Woodstock festival, and with the decline of the fairly short-lived psychodelia period, Led Zeppelin ushered in a new age of heavy rock and metal.

The 1970s

In the '70s, hard rock and psychedelic music combined to form progressive rock with notable bands being Yes, Genesis, King Crimson, and Pink Floyd.

There was definitely a sense of a 'coming of age' with bands that were evolving in the late '60s remaining strong throughout the '70s. Artists such as Led Zeppelin, The Rolling Stones and The Who travelled in private jets to sold out arenas all around the world.

Hard rock bands like Led Zeppelin influenced bands like Deep Purple to change direction and form the heavy metal movement of artists like Black Sabbath and Alice Cooper.

Queen released their first album in 1973 and would go on to dominate the next two decades with their own particular brand of rock.

The '70s were full of notable losses to the music community. Jimi Hendrix, Jim Morrison and Janis Joplin all passed away aged 27 and The Beatles split up in 1970, although all four members went on to have successful careers.

Accessible, lyrical, mainstream rock was written by artists such as Bruce Springsteen and Bob Seger and got extensive radio and TV play. Due to the proliferation of record labels and radio channels, rock continued to evolve. The '70s saw the emergence of Glam, Disco, Punk and New Wave. The late '70s heralded a new age of big hair, guitar rock with bands like Van Halen.

Recommended Listening

Rumours – Fleetwood Mac

The Wall / Animals / Wish You Were Here – Pink Floyd

Let it Be – The Beatles

Led Zeppelin III / IV / Physical Graffiti – Led Zeppelin

Queen / Queen II / Sheer Heart Attack / A Night at the Opera – Queen

Band on the Run – Wings

Machine Head – Deep Purple

Born to Run – Bruce Springsteen

Paranoid – Black Sabbath

Never Mind the Bollocks, Here's the Sex Pistols – The Sex Pistols

London Calling – The Clash

Selling England by the Pound – Genesis

Unknown Pleasures – Joy Division

Dire Straits – Dire Straits

Boston – Boston

Aja – Steely Dan

Off the Wall – Michael Jackson

Who's Next – The Who

Fragile – Yes

Dark Side of the Moon – Pink Floyd

Van Halen – Van Halen

Kiss / Alive – Kiss

(pronounced 'lĕh-'nérd 'skin-'nérd) – Lynyrd Skynyrd

Rhythm Styles

The 'stadium' rock bands such as Led Zeppelin and The Who still dominated much of the '70s, but now their riffs were harder-edged and more powerful. This first example shows how you can use pull-offs from an A chord to add movement and excitement to a simple three chord progression.

Example 9h:

Sometimes just one slightly unexpected chord can create a feeling that can last a generation. Combining this with clever off-beat phrasing adds to the power and dramatic effect of the following rhythm part.

Example 9i:

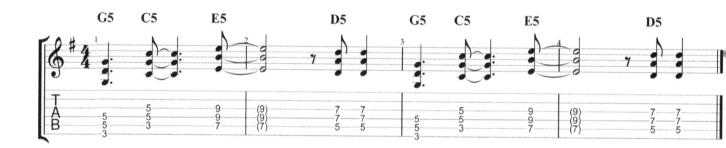

Again, tight off-beat phrasing and control combine to create a rhythm part that drives the song.

Example 9j:

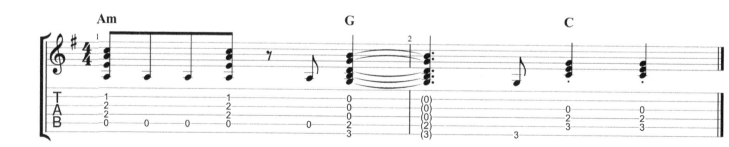

The final example teaches us a new twist on a blues shuffle. Dial in a slight crunch and play it with attitude.

Example 9k:

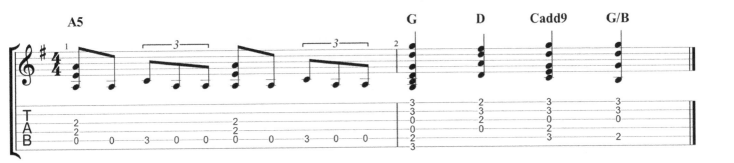

The 1980s

The early '80s saw the resurgence of hard rock with bands like Mötley Crüe finding fame after the glam period of the '70s. Heavy metal became mainstream after the breakthrough of the New Wave of British Heavy Metal (NWOBHM) with bands such as Judas Priest, Saxon and Motörhead.

As a reaction to glam, the thrash metal genre was also formed in California with bands like Metallica, Anthrax and Slayer being some of the main exponents.

Guns N' Roses exploded on to the scene with *Appetite for Destruction* in 1987 and dominated the charts with their unique approach to accessible hard rock.

The success of bands like Van Halen, Queen and AC/DC spanned a decade that also saw the comeback of artists such as Alice Cooper and Aerosmith. The 1980s was also the decade of 'The Guitar Virtuoso' with players such as Eddie Van Halen, Joe Satriani, Steve Vai and Randy Rhoads gaining widespread acclaim.

Of the post-punk movement, important artists include The Cure and The Smiths, who moved away from the dark sonic territory of the punk movement and added lyrical sophistication.

Instrumentally, the '80s saw more influence of synths and digital instruments and a proliferation of digital recording techniques allowing greater use of multi-tracking and studio effects.

Recommended Listening

Brothers in Arms – Dire Straits

Born in the USA – Bruce Springsteen

Synchronicity – The Police

Slippery When Wet – Bon Jovi

Hysteria – Def Leppard

The Queen is Dead – The Smiths

5150 / 1984 – Van Halen

Appetite for *Destruction* – Guns N' Roses

Ace of Spades – Motörhead

Master of Puppets – Metallica

Among the Living – Anthrax

Surfing with the Alien – Joe Satriani

Passion and Warfare – Steve Vai (1990)

Extreme – Extreme

Greatest Hits / A Kind of Magic – Queen

Blizzard of Ozz / Diary of a Madman / The Ultimate Sin – Ozzy Osbourne

Back in Black – AC/DC

Licensed to Ill – The Beastie Boys

Too Fast for Love / Shout at the Devil / Dr Feelgood – Mötley Crüe

Whitesnake / Slide it in – Whitesnake

The Unforgettable Fire / War / The Joshua Tree – U2

Rhythm Styles

Chords were often played as rhythmic stabs in an otherwise static harmony. The following example uses the slash chords seen on page 71 to create harmonic movements over an A pedal tone. Keep the open strings muted and let the chords pop out.

Example 9l:

84

Rock bands like Van Halen, Whitesnake and Extreme often used the following addition to the Major barre chord to add some movement to the rhythm part. Think of these shapes like extended power chords and add the extra note with your 4th finger.

Example 9m:

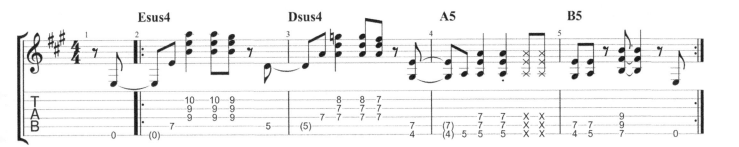

Sometimes it only takes a few chords to announce a major comeback. This next rhythm part in the style of AC/DC combines a catchy lead fill with three simple power chords.

Example 9n:

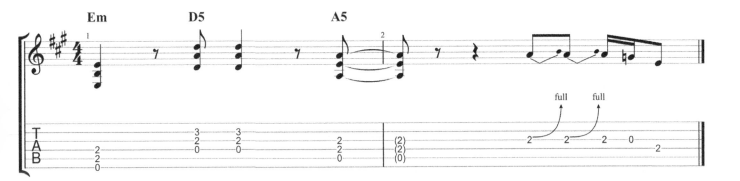

The 1990s

The early '90s was dominated by the sound of grunge, a musical movement formed in Seattle as a way to reclaim rock music from the virtuoso performances of the '80s. The most important artists were Nirvana, Pearl Jam and Alice in Chains, and all these bands taught a generation that you didn't need to be Eddie Van Halen to play the guitar.

'Alternative' rock bands achieved mainstream success and The Red Hot Chili Peppers fused funk ideas with a rock aesthetic to become one of the most important bands of the decade.

In the UK, Britpop was influenced by the British bands of the '60s and '70s, and once again spoke of a youth counterculture. Oasis released the second biggest-selling UK album of all time with *(What's the Story) Morning Glory*.

Recommended Listening

Nevermind / In Utero – Nirvana

Ten / Vs – Pearl Jam

Metallica (The Black Album) – Metallica

Dookie – Green Day

Blood Sugar Sex Magik / Californication – Red Hot Chili Peppers

(What's the Story) Morning Glory – Oasis

Superunknown – Soundgarden

Rage Against the Machine / Evil Empire – Rage Against the Machine

Follow the Leader – Korn

Ænima – Tool

OK Computer / The Bends – Radiohead

Weezer – Weezer

Urban Hymns – The Verve

Use Your Illusion I / II – Guns N' Roses

Grace – Jeff Buckley

Make Yourself / S.C.I.E.N.C.E. – Incubus

Sublime – Sublime

Parklife – Blur

Everything Must Go – Manic Street Preachers

Different Class – Pulp

The Stone Roses – The Stone Roses (1989)

Pills 'n' Thrills and Bellyaches – The Happy Mondays

Vulgar Display of Power / Cowboys from Hell – Pantera

Foo Fighters – Foo Fighters

Significant Other – Limp Bizkit

Doolittle – Pixies (1989)

Rhythm Styles

Grunge was less about instrumental ability and more about the message that music was for the people. The first example uses simple power chords and a straight rhythm feel to pack a punch while allowing the vocal message to get through.

Example 9o:

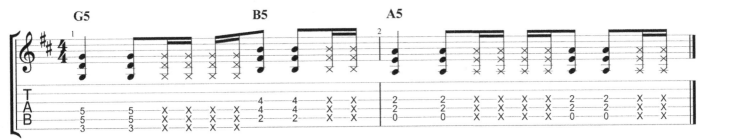

Rock in the '90s was often formed from catchy, repetitive phrases that used simple chords and rhythms.

Example 9p:

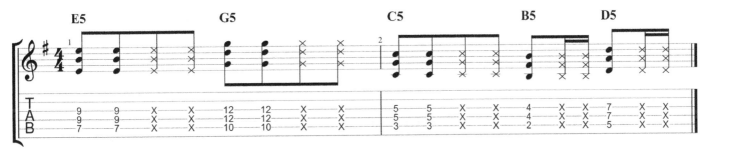

This next example is a bit more on the poppy side so use a clean tone and lots of pick attack. The following rhythm figure is based on one of the biggest selling songs of 1991. Once again, notice how the rock hammer on has been repurposed into a funky riff.

Example 9q:

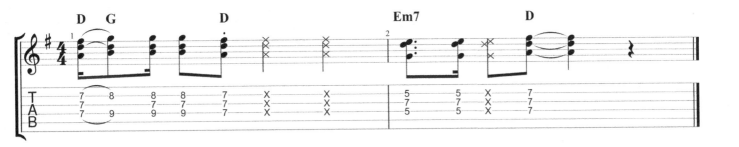

Britpop owed a lot to the bands of the '60s and '70s, in particular The Beatles. The following example uses held notes over a descending bassline to build an anthemic track.

Example 9r:

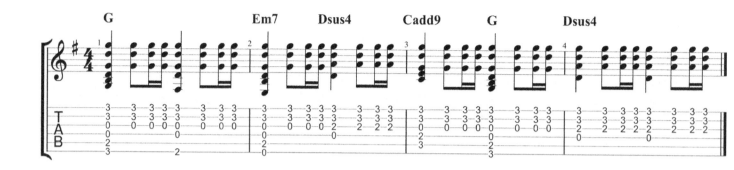

The 2000s

Into the 2000s and the Internet was a driving force in music promotion and discovery. Because artists could now distribute music freely without the need for record labels, a definite fragmentation of genres started to occur. It was also easier for artists to find inspiration from new influences.

Outside of the US, Britpop was still extremely popular, although by the end of the decade bands were eager to lose their Britpop label, labelling themselves as 'post-Britpop' despite still drawing influence from bands like The Rolling Stones and The Beatles.

Alternative rock and other genres of hard rock, such as nu metal, post-grunge and emo flourished out of older more established genres. In the middle of the decade there was a slight revival of power rock, spearheaded by bands like The Darkness.

In heavier rock styles, seven-string guitars were now commonplace after becoming more mainstream in the late '90s through bands like Korn and Limp Bizkit.

Recommended Listening

Continuum – John Mayer

Black Holes and Revelations – Muse

Bleed American – Jimmy Eat World

This Is It – The Strokes

Audioslave – Audioslave

Lateralus – Tool

American Idiot – Green Day

Permission to Land – The Darkness

X & Y – Coldplay

Echo Park – Feeder

In Your Honor / One by One – Foo Fighters

City of Evil / Waking the Fallen – Avenged Sevenfold

The Green Album – Weezer

Employment – Kaiser Chiefs

In Keeping Secrets of Silent Earth: 3 – Coheed and Cambria

From Under The Cork Tree – Fall Out Boy

Take Off Your Pants and Jacket – Blink-182

Songs for the Deaf – Queens of the Stone Age

Funeral – Arcade Fire

White Blood Cells / Elephant – The White Stripes

Toxicity – System of a Down

Reinventing the Steel – Pantera

The Black Parade – My Chemical Romance

Rhythm Styles

These examples focus on the more accessible side of rock. If you want to go a bit darker, check out the book **Heavy Metal Rhythm Guitar** by Rob Thorpe. At the turn of the millennium rock music was incredibly diverse so consider the following examples just the tip of the iceberg.

Keep the first example tight, staccato and aggressive. Imagine each full chord as a sledgehammer knocking down a stone wall.

Example 9s:

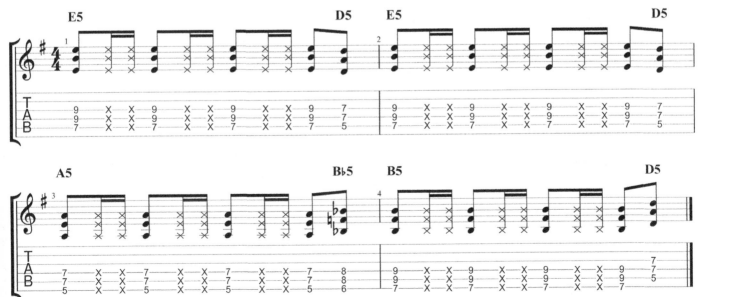

The following example was inspired by Green Day's powerful riffing so play it fast and loud. Notice how just one off-beat push on the D5 chord sets up a chain of events that doesn't resolve until halfway through the next bar.

Example 9t:

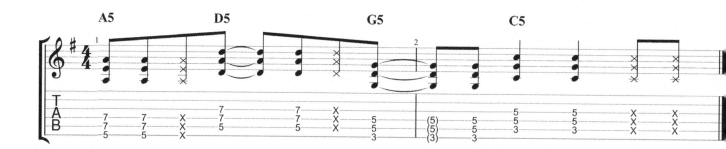

The next example is a *You Really Got Me* for a new generation. Driving, syncopated power chords and a catchy hook lick draw it all together.

Example 9u:

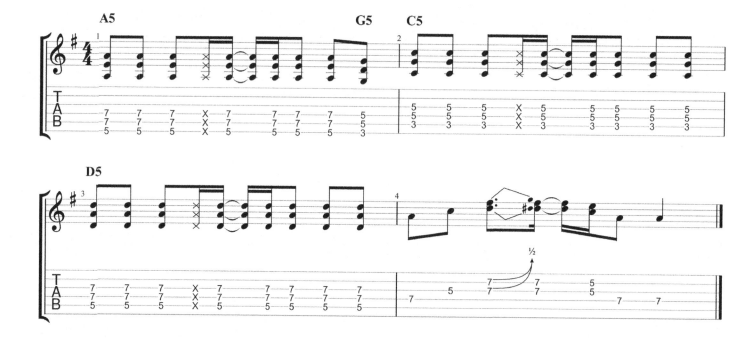

This final example combines barre chord fragments with a small repetitious embellishment to create a floaty, memorable rhythm part that creates a great counter to a busy vocal melody.

Example 9v:

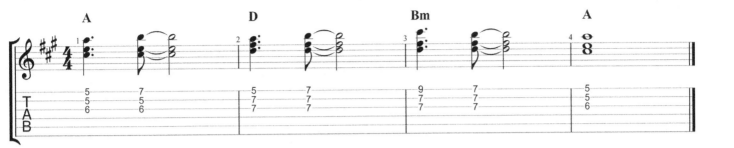

The 2010s

This decade has been dominated by rock bands like Foo Fighters, Avenged Sevenfold, Bullet for my Valentine and Fall Out Boy. However, there has also been a resurgence of some of the biggest names in rock, such as AC/DC and Van Halen.

Generally speaking, lighter 'pop' rock owes a lot to the grunge bands of the '90s whereas heavier rock guitar parts still use many power chord ideas that are similar in style to the 'hair' bands of the '80s. However, rock is now more diverse than it has ever been, with a sub-genre to suit every taste. I can't hope to come close to covering every style here, but some important ideas are contained below.

Recommended Listening

The Suburbs / Reflektor – Arcade Fire

Suck It and See – Arctic Monkeys

Wasting Light / Sonic Highways – Foo Fighters

El Camino / Turn Blue – The Black Keys

Hail to the King – Avenged Sevenfold

Culture Clash – The Aristocrats

MBV – My Bloody Valentine

...Like Clockwork – Queens of the Stone Age

Modern Vampires of the City – Vampire Weekend

Wrecking Ball – Bruce Springsteen

Rhythm Styles

A heavier power chord example kicks off this decade: pay careful attention to the muted scratches and keep the muting tight in the strumming hand.

Example 9w:

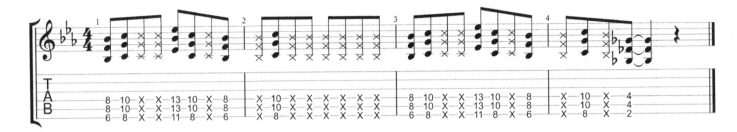

Watch out for the shuffle feel of this next riff. Play the chords slightly straighter in the second four bars to recreate an anthemic riff.

Example 9x:

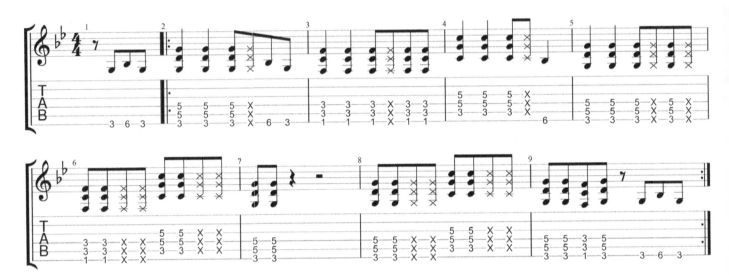

Here's another riff with a lot of syncopation that shows the 1960s' roots of modern rock.

Example 9y:

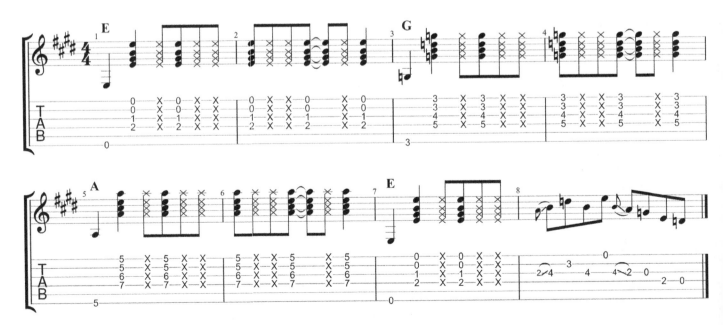

Conclusions and Practice Advice

In this book I have tried to give you the tools needed to become a confident, accurate and competent rock rhythm guitar player. If you have worked through the first part of this book, then you are well on your way to being able to play any rhythm that you can conceive. Make sure you keep coming back to these exercises, as our sense of rhythm can sometimes get a bit sloppy over time.

One useful practice idea is to use the exercises in Part One as a quick warm up each day before you start your practice. Even just taking ten minutes to focus on rhythm before you start to play will have a far-reaching and positive effect on the rest of the practice you do in that session.

Guitarists often get so distracted by scales, arpeggios and lead guitar concepts that we often forget that 'the right note played at the wrong time is still a wrong note'. Developing a conscious control of your rhythmic placement will enable you to use any other musical concepts much more fluently. Building a strong sense of rhythm was definitely the part of my development that allowed me to hear that often guitarists are using simple ideas – they're just playing them with impeccable timing.

Always practice with a combination of backing tracks and a metronome. Backing tracks can be more fun as they give you more of a groove to work with, but stripping everything right back to just a simple click makes you work harder to develop your own sense of time.

As your sense of time improves, try halving the metronome speed and hearing the click as beats two and four of the bar. As you have to fill in the one and three yourself, you are forced to concentrate more, which in turn develops your sense of rhythm further. Eventually, you might be able to practice with the click only on beat four.

As a modern guitarist, rhythmic accuracy is one of the most important skills that you can develop. Having control of what and *when* you play will make you a valuable player in any band situation. Sometimes it seems like everyone wants to play lead guitar, but the truth is that being a versatile and creative rhythm guitar player will open many more doors for you.

The one thing that is really hard to teach is *creativity,* but I believe that the more we learn about other people's music, the more we will absorb. All these ideas then get combined in our subconscious and eventually come out as our own distinctive voice.

If you are getting stuck writing your own riffs and rhythm parts, set yourself the task of writing a part 'in the style of' a particular guitarist. Listen deeply to their rhythmic ideas and treat your troublesome chord progression in the same way. If you do this exercise and model your playing on three or four different guitarists, I can guarantee that you will come up with something original and personal after a short amount of time.

Experimentation is always the key, and working with other musicians helps. In music, the whole is usually greater than the sum of its parts and this idea applies to creativity too. If you're writing songs, get a few musicians in a room together and allow them free rein to get creative with your ideas. Don't be isolated and try to write everything yourself, but make sure that you've practiced enough to be able to play anything that comes up in the writing session, even if it takes a few minutes.

Listen to everything you can, both in and out of your chosen genre. The more you listen to, the more you will find to play. Your brain will become a big melting pot of musical ideas and you will always have something to say on your instrument.

I believe it is also important to find a few minutes to listen to music you *don't* like as long as you're analytical about what it is you find offensive. Remember, many chord progressions get used time and time again in all forms of music, so be clear what it is you don't like. For example, it could be the melody, the production, the guitar tone or the bassline… the list goes on.

The other side of occasionally listening to music you don't like is that sometimes there is a great idea that you can lift and 're-purpose' for your own needs. Maybe that Justin Bieber middle section would work better restyled into your nu metal masterpiece?!

With only a limited range of common chords, musicians borrow from one another all the time, often unconsciously. Never plagiarise, but it is OK to allow yourself to be inspired by the works of others. Transcribing the music of others is one of the quickest ways to master your instrument.

Music allows us to find a voice, and it should always be a positive experience for all involved. If nothing else, make sure you enjoy what you do.

Have fun!

Joseph

Appendix: Advanced Rhythm Exercises

The following pages contain the more advanced rhythm exercises from Part One of this book to allow you to balance the technical and musical examples more easily. They are included as audio downloads with their original track numbers.

Advanced Examples from Chapter Four

There are five other important rhythmic groupings that combine two 1/16th notes and two 1/16th note rests. We will cover them here for completeness, although by now you are probably starting to figure out these permutations by yourself.

We will look at each grouping in turn, and study a rhythmic example for each one. These examples do get gradually more difficult, but if you take them slowly and always keep your strumming hand moving in time, you will quickly master them. As always, listen and play along with the audio. Your progress will improve dramatically.

Learn the following examples in the same way as you learnt the earlier ones. Begin with fully muted strums before playing single muted notes and finally adding static, followed by changing power chords.

Example 4q:

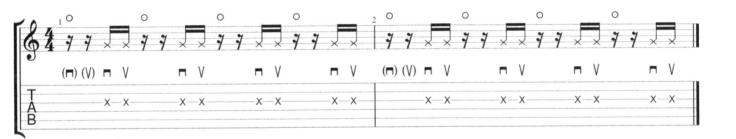

Example 4r:

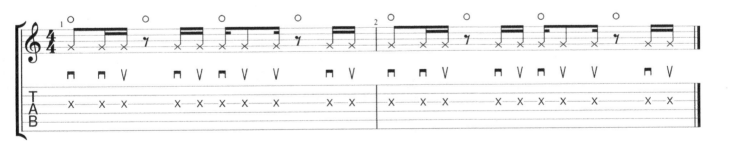

Example 4s:

Example 4t:

Example 4u:

Example 4v:

Example 4w:

Example 4x:

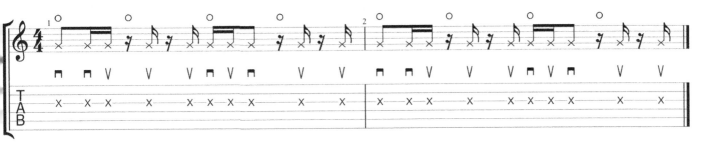

Example 4y:

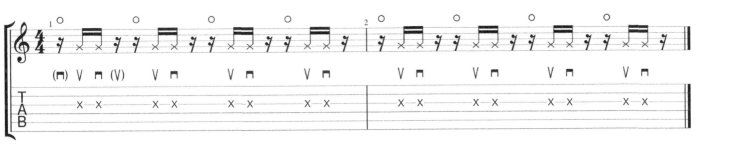

Example 4z:

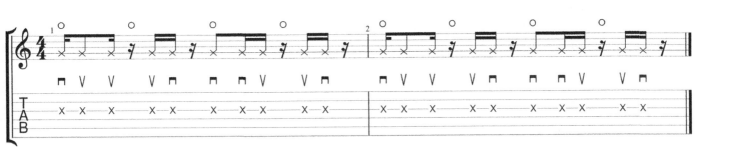

Advanced Examples from Chapter Five

To test your skills, here are some extremely sparse rhythmic parts to try.

As you start to master them, try playing them along with backing track one before advancing to the quicker backing tracks.

Begin with muted strums before moving to an E5 chord and then using chord sequences.

Example 5k:

Example 5l:

Example 5m:

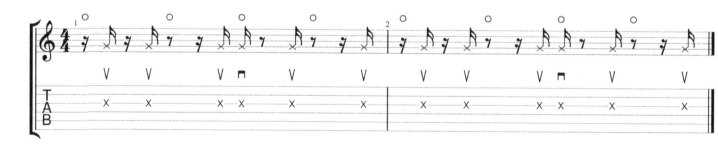

Create as many of these kinds of rhythms as you can. You could start by writing rhythms arbitrarily and randomly combining different 1/16th note rhythms

The ability to play sparse chord stabs will set you apart as an excellent rock rhythm guitar player. Practice each rhythm both with backing tracks and your metronome. It is easier to practice with a backing track, but you will have to work harder and become more self-reliant if you just use a metronome. Ideally combine both approaches.

Made in the USA
Las Vegas, NV
23 January 2022

42107805R00057